This is what I know:

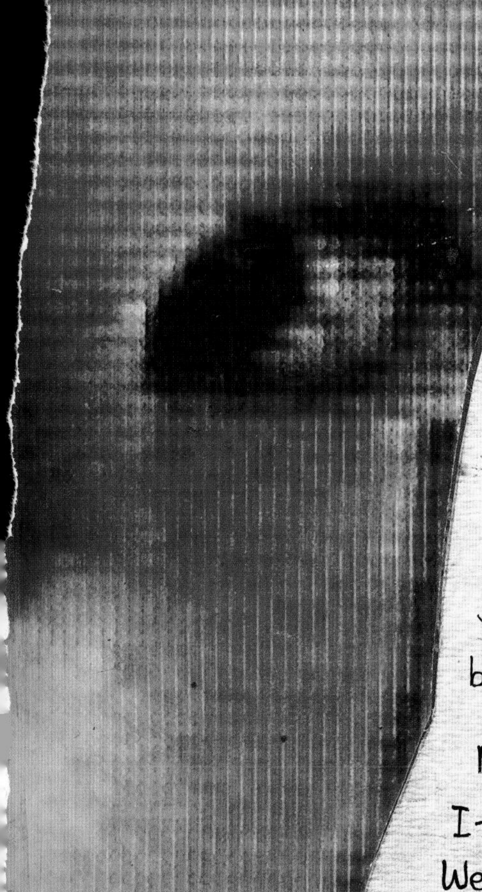

I am looking for a boy who might look like my father. Light eyes, brown hair, and small hands. A smile that might curl downward. Sometimes I'm told he was put in an oven, and sometimes I'm told he was shot in the head.

They were put on a train. By then just the two of them were traveling together, a woman and her son. It must have been July or August, when the last transports took place. They were in a wooden boxcar with no windows, the car crowded with people. Each had hidden money, jewelry, photographs, medicine, books, musical instruments, food, and everything else. In pockets, the lining of jackets, in the backs of their mouths.

They arrived. Everyone was ordered out of the boxcar and made to form two lines.

He was put into the other line.

My grandmother's son.

I-Z-H-O-U.

We are the same age. Nine. I am looking for him at night with a plastic magnifying glass in my father's study. It is a room with artifacts from faraway places: rugs from Istanbul, teak camels from Egypt, a rock from the Gaza Strip, porcelain opium pipes from Laos. The study is an airport where you can be led by books and objects to other places, events, and people. It smells of rubber cement. Mostly, though, it is the hundreds of books on the Holocaust that envelop the study. I search through countless pictures of Auschwitz. Pixilated shades of gray and black, rows of men with torsos like tree branches about to snap. In front of wooden boxcars, I see old men hunched in black overcoats and women with eyes fixed on smoke in the sky. Turn the page. Is that him? The boy in the left bunk, eyes like black tourmalines?

HOTEL
UKRAIN

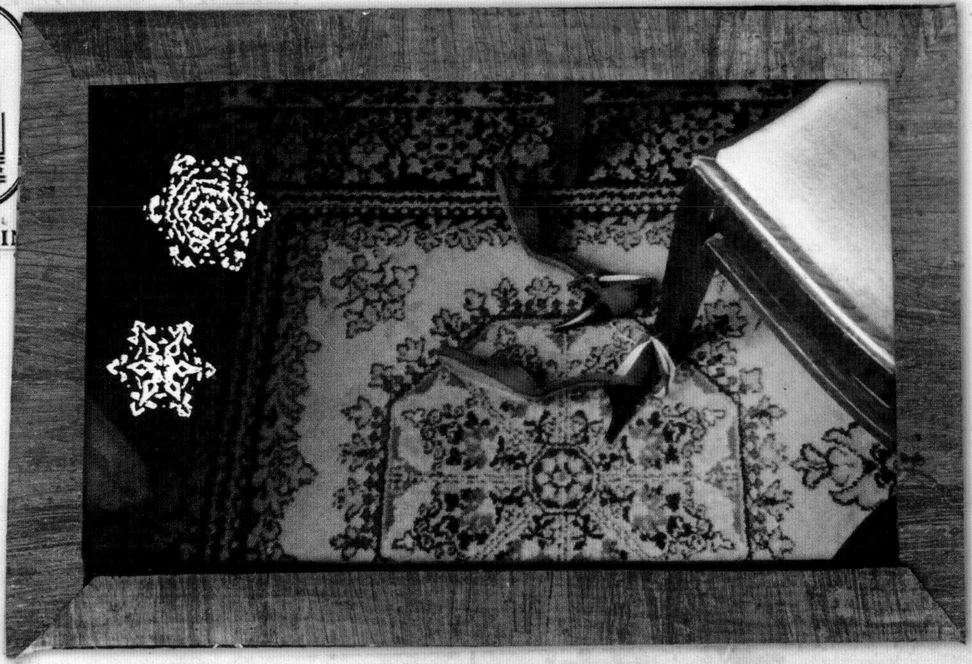

Snow falling in air that smells like boiled wool. Icy stars that fade on my face.

Moscow. The Ukraina Hotel.

Scraped hardwood floors and a rug from Turkmenistan that is threadbare in the middle. The light through the window is turning blue. I sit on my bed and trace a finger over the little camera. A silver dent came, maybe, from the overnight train many years before. The camera slid out of my pocket as my friend fell asleep on our bunk, darkness and light from outside painting our faces like tigers. Another dent reminds me of my grandmother Reni Lazarov's stainless steel pots, large and scratched from decades of use. Ours is the familiar story: the Jewish grandparents who survived the war, all that history that has become like white noise. The pots are vessels of meaning for my grandmother. The dents are little maps. Secrets.

This room is romantic. The type of room where you would meet a lover and watch the snowfall, that rare kind of encounter where silence pounds heavy on your heart.

2/1 Kutuzovsky prospect, Moscow, Russia Telephone: +7 (495) 933-68-01 Fax: +7 (495) 933-68-39

In the lobby bar of the Ukraina, jet-lagged and bleary-eyed, I watch a man. He wears Casual Friday clothes, as though he works for a computer company. Strips of blond hair smear across his forehead. His eyes eat the sex worker who moves through the room stroking her damp fur coat with stubby nails. He aches with regret as she walks past him.

There is something sad and revealed about the man. I want to tell this man that I have no idea what I'm doing. That I'm scared and I'm so sorry. That my father begged me not to go and to come home to Toronto instead. He asked the obvious question.

Why are you doing this?

Because when I was a kid, I could see the lake from my parents' garden, and now it's obscured by smog. Because sometimes I think that the world is dying, melting, and forgetting. And why doesn't anyone send handwritten letters anymore? I need to tell the man in the lobby bar that these problems gather and one day might overwhelm you ... maybe you stop eating meat, quit your job, go to India and live in an ashram; or you take drugs, spend too much money, fuck too many random strangers, or just disconnect from your life.

Now my money belt is stuck to my stomach with sweat. Inside the belt are envelopes filled with money for expenses. I have separated everything into categories: food, lodging, car rental, gas, etc. This is an attempt to convince myself that I know what I'm doing. I want to tell the man that I have taken out an emergency evacuation life-insurance policy, that I have packed too many clothes. That on the morning of the flight to Moscow I moved my bonsai to the windowsill. I also dusted my picture frames and tightened the lids of my cleaning products. I don't know how to work my tape recorder ... how to take a Polaroid ... how to speak, actually.

I stand up to leave, walk to the elevator, press the button.

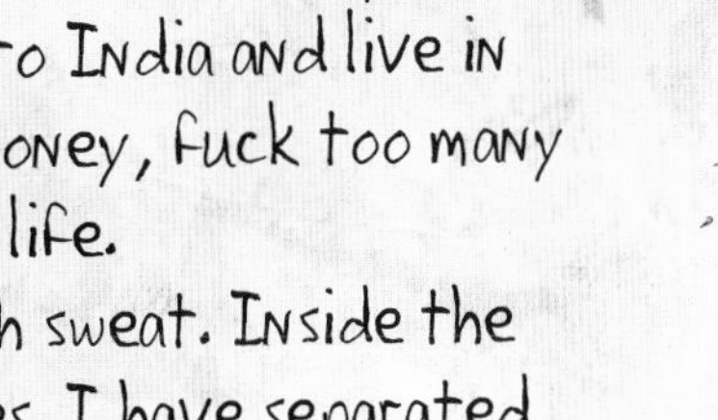

2/1 Kutuzovsky prospect, Moscow, Russia Telephone: +7 (495) 933-68-01 Fax: +7 (495) 933-68-39

Nazran. The Hotel Assa.

I walked until dusk. A first dusk for me in Ingushetia. My first day in a refugee camp wasn't what I expected. I had images in my head of Sudan or Afghanistan: wind, dust, and silence. This was like an ordinary village anywhere in the world. Waterproof tents lined walkways while girls in acrylic dresses ran past, playing. Wide Caspian faces and waxy skin. I turned a corner onto an empty pathway, my cameras and art supplies heavy on my back. A boy of about 19 stood in the doorway of a tent. He looked at my bag and moved toward me. I froze.

This story was running though my mind: In October 1998, three Britons and a New Zealander - Peter Kennedy, Darren Hickey, Rudolph Petschi, and Stanley Shaw - were taken hostage in Chechnya while working to install a phone network. After a botched rescue attempt, their severed heads were found on a roadside. What would lead one person to do this to another? When I arrived at the Nazran airport today, a group of armed guards was waiting to meet me. Every journalist and human rights organization I spoke to had strongly advised that I travel only in the company of armed guards, but as soon as I saw these greasy, pockmarked men, who looked at my tits while their AK-47s dangled like shopping bags, I didn't want them there.

As the young man walked toward me on the pathway, I saw the possibilities of his violence and rage. The man looked at my bag. He was pointing. "You dropped your pens, look -"

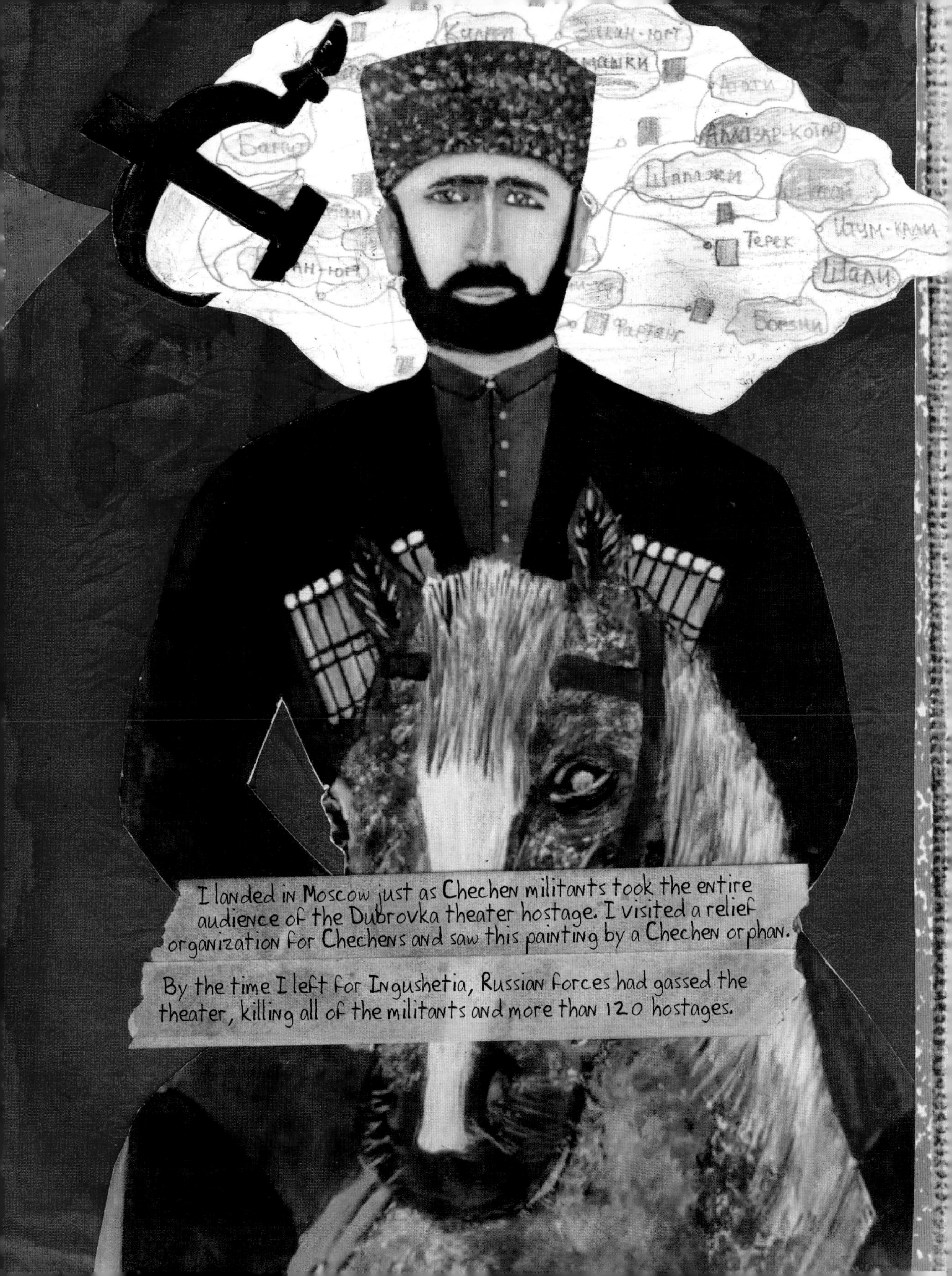
I landed in Moscow just as Chechen militants took the entire audience of the Dubrovka theater hostage. I visited a relief organization for Chechens and saw this painting by a Chechen orphan.
By the time I left for Ingushetia, Russian forces had gassed the theater, killing all of the militants and more than 120 hostages.

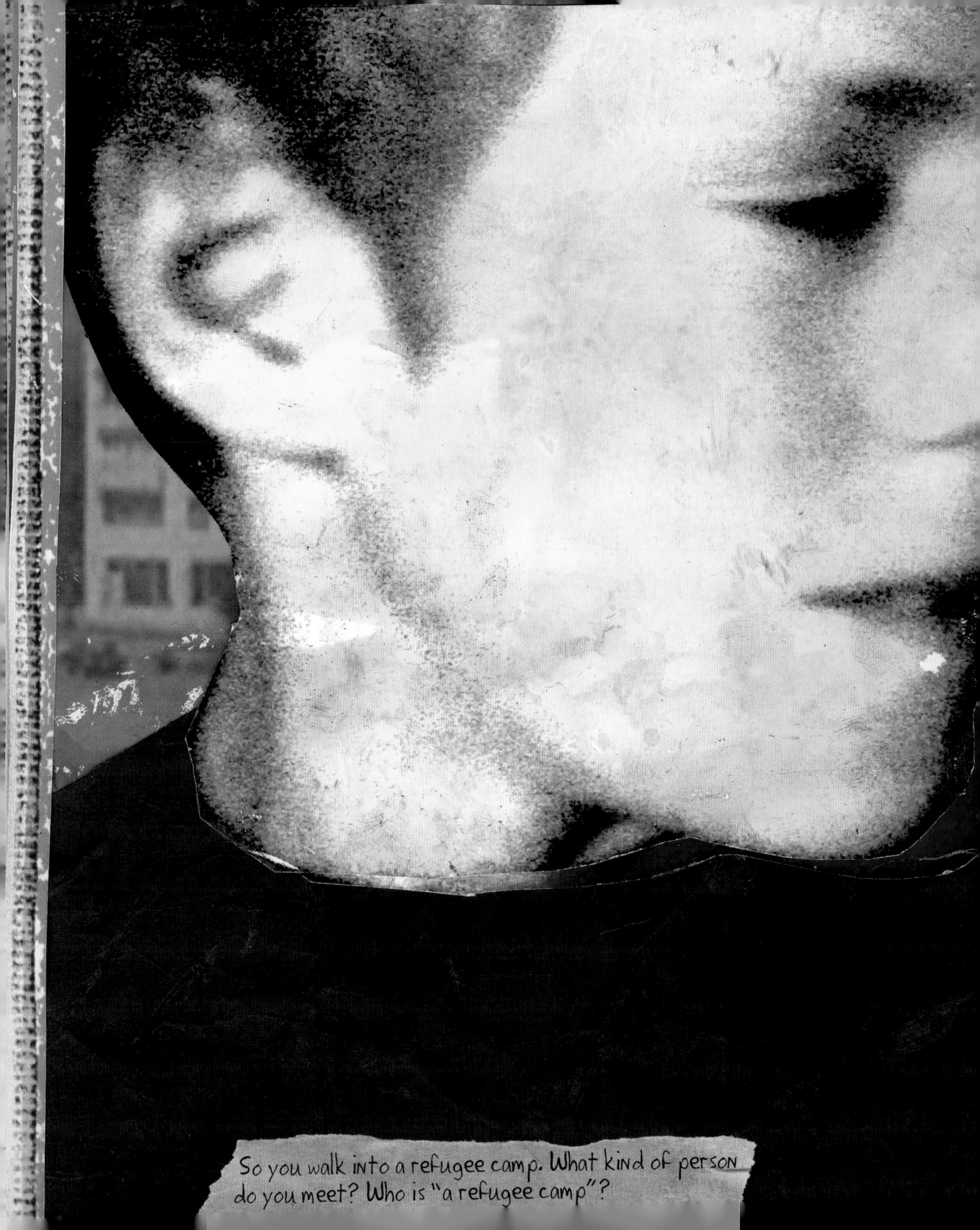
So you walk into a refugee camp. What kind of person do you meet? Who is "a refugee camp"?

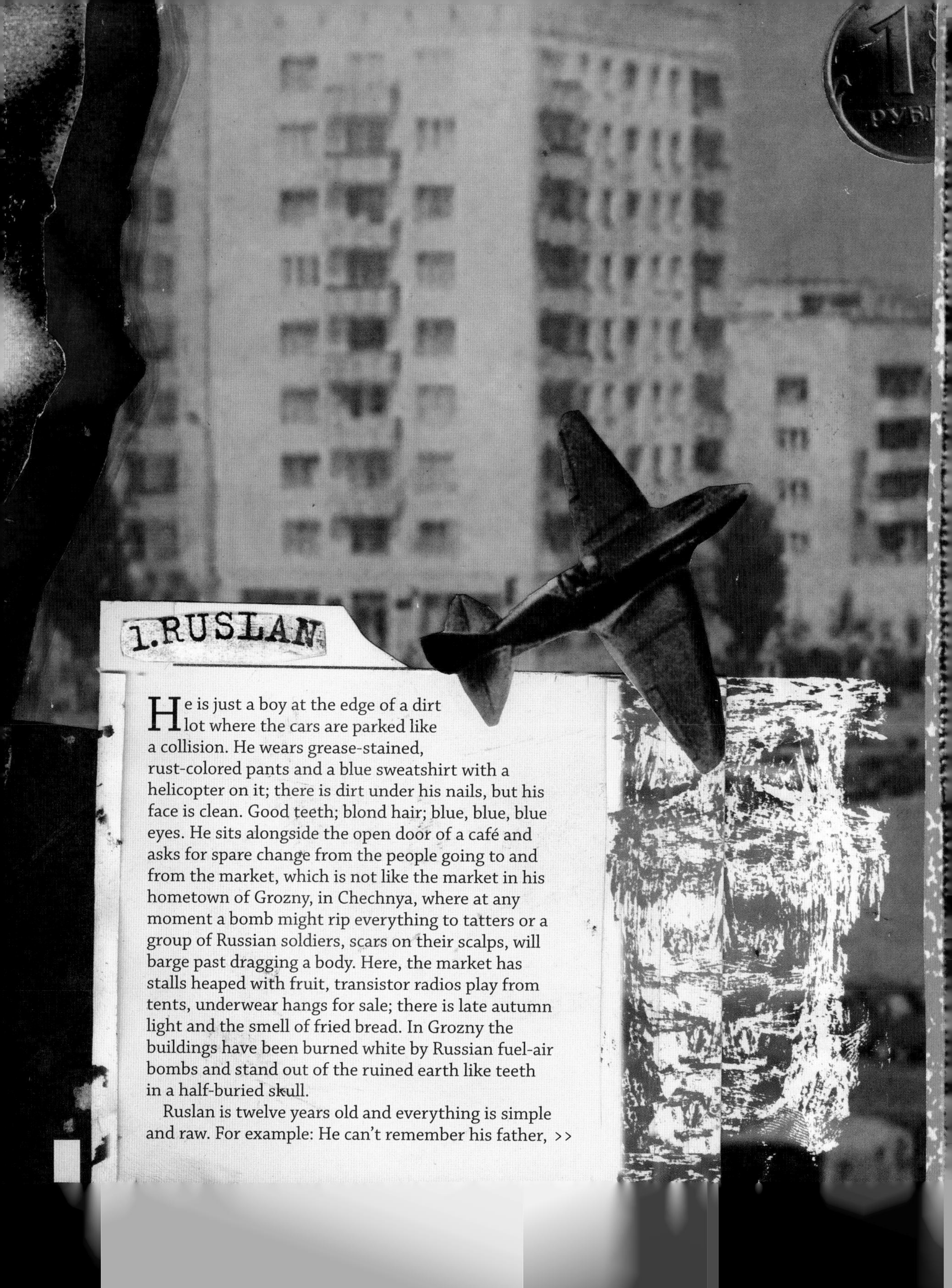

1. RUSLAN

He is just a boy at the edge of a dirt lot where the cars are parked like a collision. He wears grease-stained, rust-colored pants and a blue sweatshirt with a helicopter on it; there is dirt under his nails, but his face is clean. Good teeth; blond hair; blue, blue, blue eyes. He sits alongside the open door of a café and asks for spare change from the people going to and from the market, which is not like the market in his hometown of Grozny, in Chechnya, where at any moment a bomb might rip everything to tatters or a group of Russian soldiers, scars on their scalps, will barge past dragging a body. Here, the market has stalls heaped with fruit, transistor radios play from tents, underwear hangs for sale; there is late autumn light and the smell of fried bread. In Grozny the buildings have been burned white by Russian fuel-air bombs and stand out of the ruined earth like teeth in a half-buried skull.

Ruslan is twelve years old and everything is simple and raw. For example: He can't remember his father, >>

only that he found his father's body, exploded by a missile, in their house in Grozny. Then Ruslan's mother gathered him to go, that instant, only him and a few precious things. Ruslan, who in another life would be a high school quarterback or captain of the debate team, or both; the type who would go on to business school and marry a real estate agent and be jowly from the soft life by the age of thirty-five. If he lived near the coast, he might surf; otherwise, he would shoot skeet. Square jawed. Maybe the kind of kid you don't particularly like, who might have made your own childhood a torment with his effortless self-assurance and sense of superiority, a boy to whom everything comes too easily. Only, though, in another life.

According to what Ruslan was told, she was walking along a road in the camp when she was hit by a car and killed. They say she was drunk. His mother. But he doesn't like to talk about things that make him unhappy. ✛

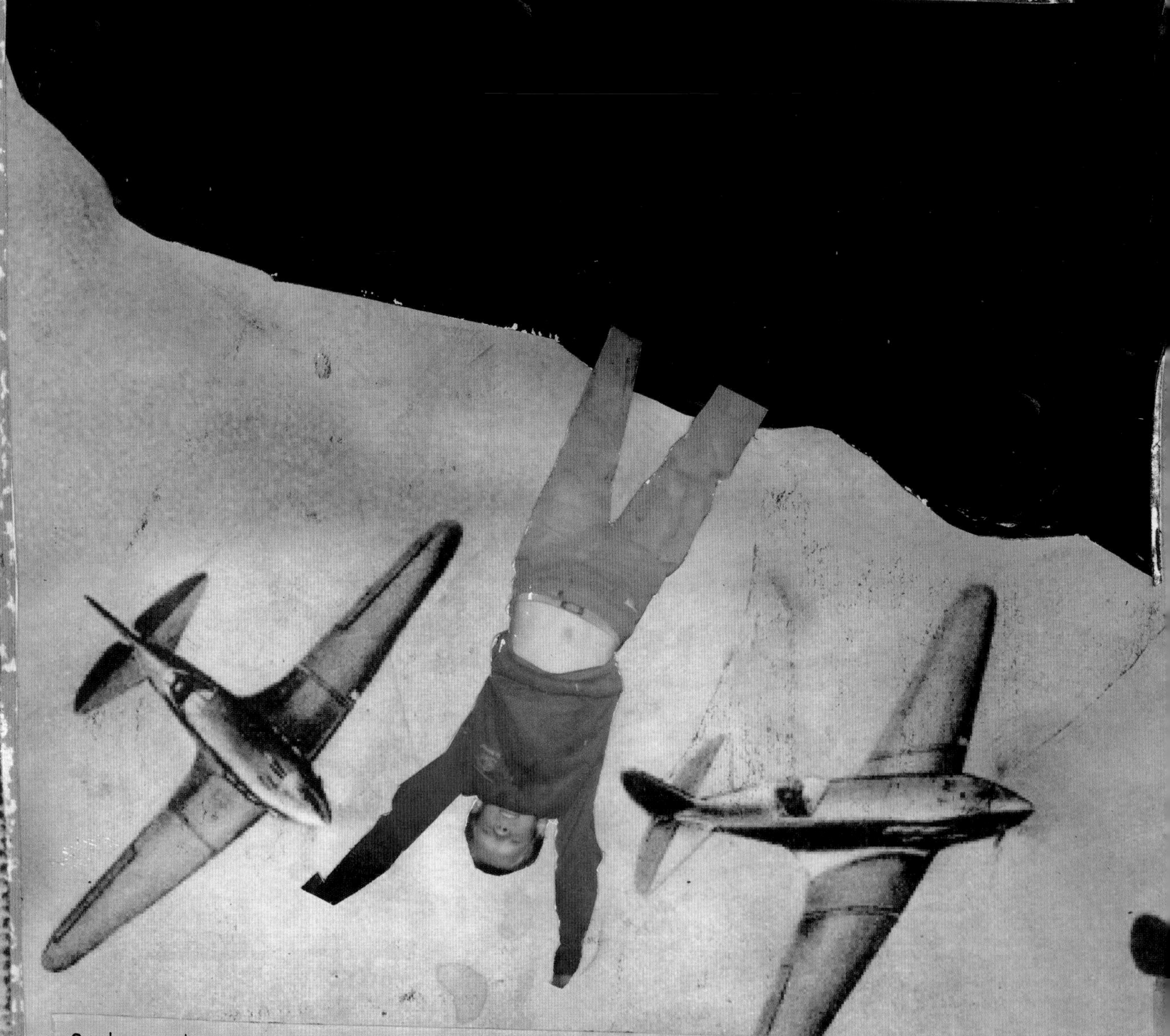

Ruslan took hundreds of photos. I lent him a camera. He said he liked taking pictures of details - the sky and the clouds and his nails.

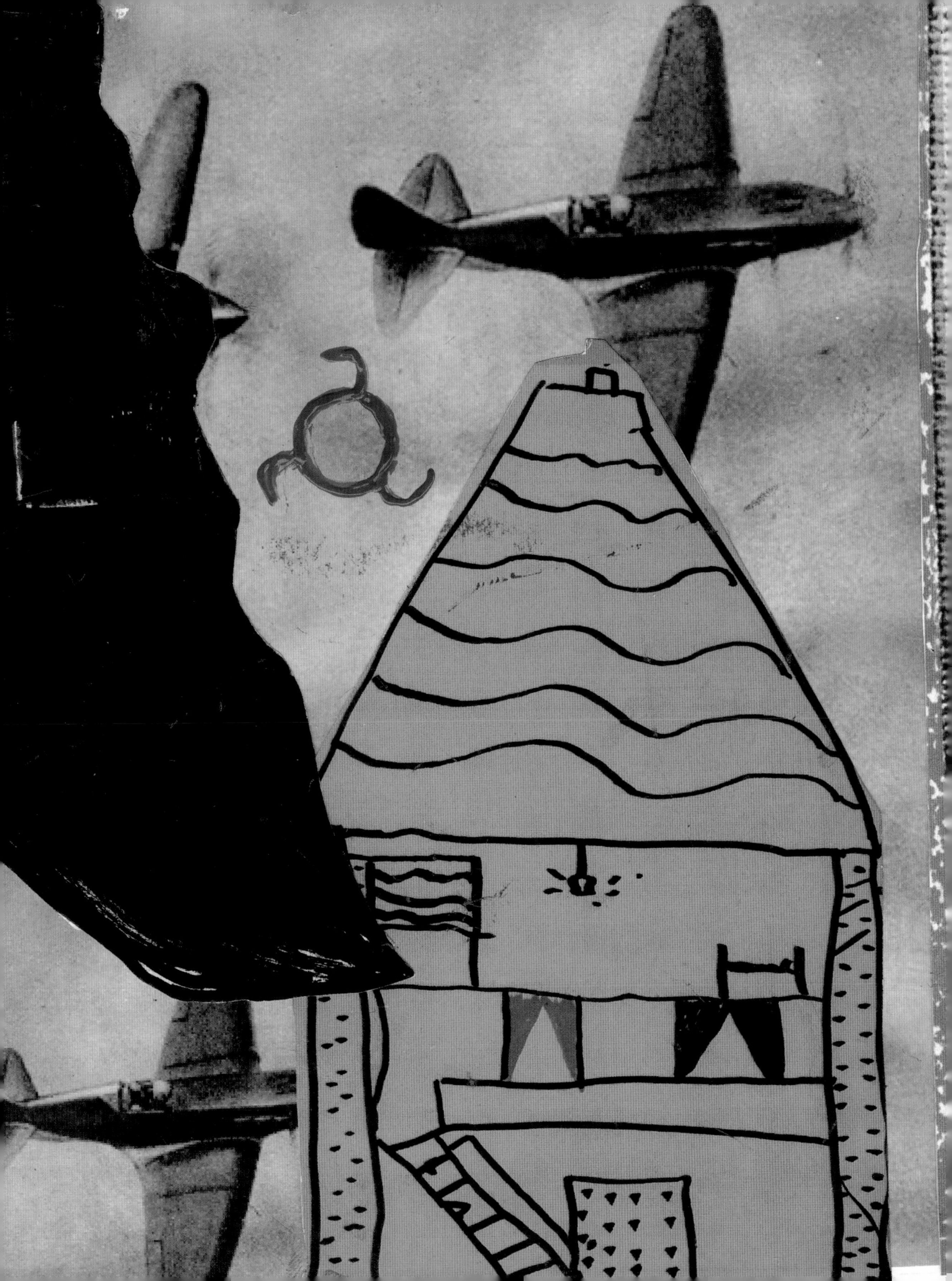

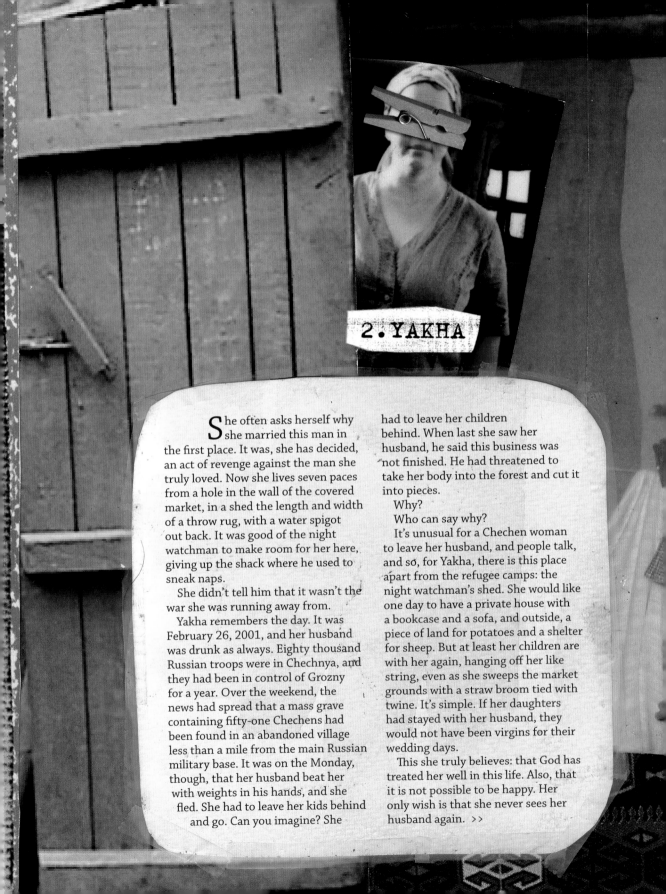

2. YAKHA

She often asks herself why she married this man in the first place. It was, she has decided, an act of revenge against the man she truly loved. Now she lives seven paces from a hole in the wall of the covered market, in a shed the length and width of a throw rug, with a water spigot out back. It was good of the night watchman to make room for her here, giving up the shack where he used to sneak naps.

She didn't tell him that it wasn't the war she was running away from.

Yakha remembers the day. It was February 26, 2001, and her husband was drunk as always. Eighty thousand Russian troops were in Chechnya, and they had been in control of Grozny for a year. Over the weekend, the news had spread that a mass grave containing fifty-one Chechens had been found in an abandoned village less than a mile from the main Russian military base. It was on the Monday, though, that her husband beat her with weights in his hands, and she fled. She had to leave her kids behind and go. Can you imagine? She had to leave her children behind. When last she saw her husband, he said this business was not finished. He had threatened to take her body into the forest and cut it into pieces.

Why?

Who can say why?

It's unusual for a Chechen woman to leave her husband, and people talk, and so, for Yakha, there is this place apart from the refugee camps: the night watchman's shed. She would like one day to have a private house with a bookcase and a sofa, and outside, a piece of land for potatoes and a shelter for sheep. But at least her children are with her again, hanging off her like string, even as she sweeps the market grounds with a straw broom tied with twine. It's simple. If her daughters had stayed with her husband, they would not have been virgins for their wedding days.

This she truly believes: that God has treated her well in this life. Also, that it is not possible to be happy. Her only wish is that she never sees her husband again. >>

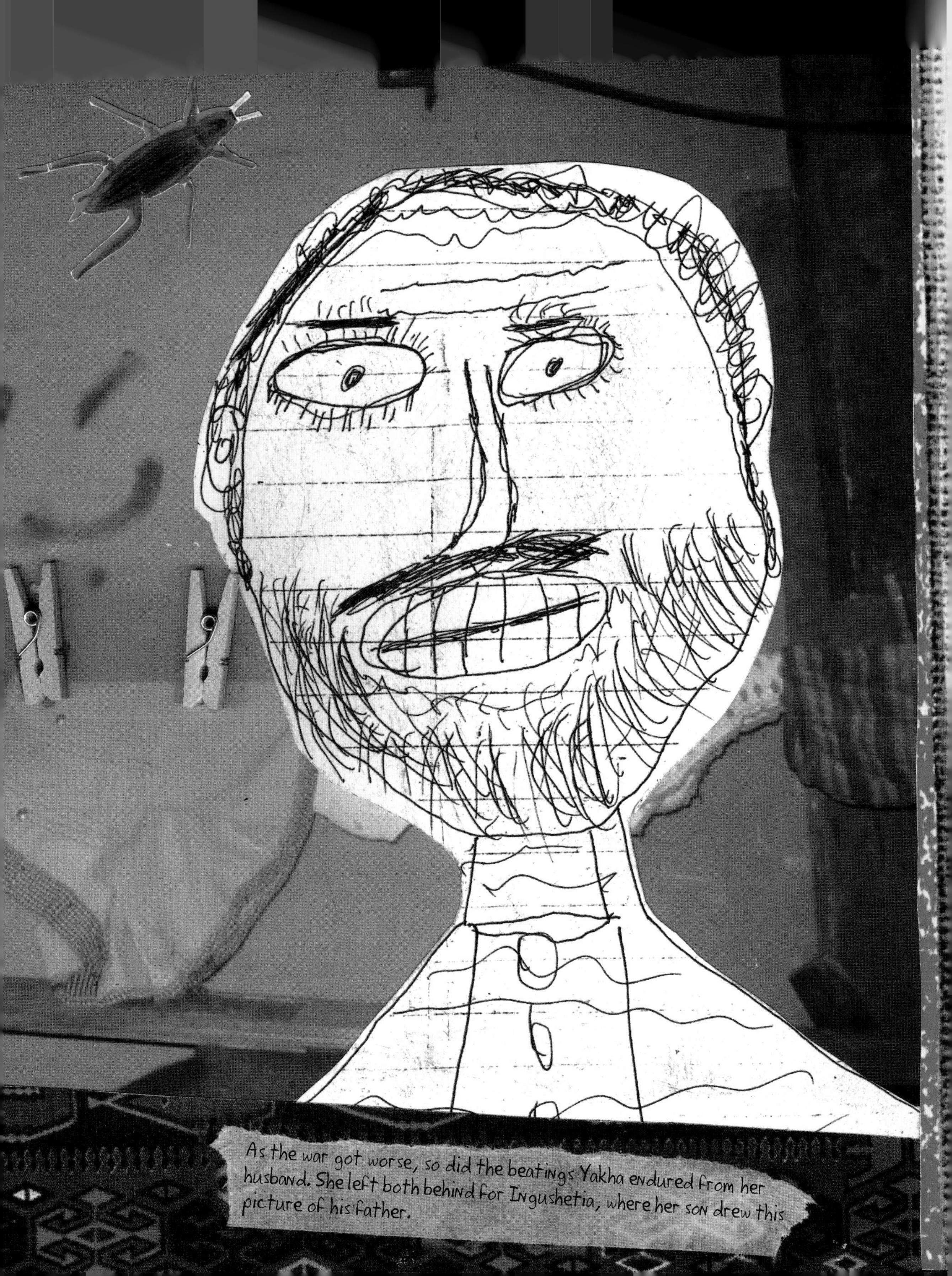

As the war got worse, so did the beatings Yakha endured from her husband. She left both behind for Ingushetia, where her son drew this picture of his father.

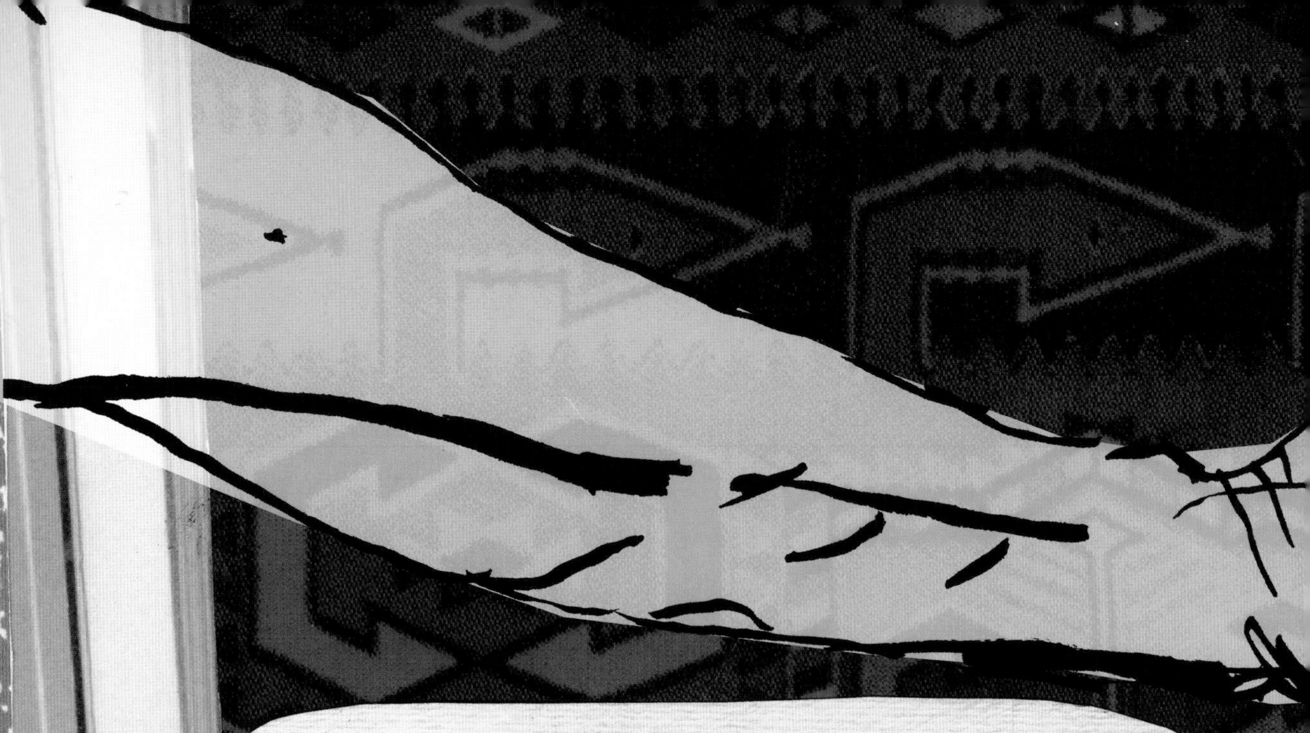

Then her husband is standing in the doorway. It happens just like that—nine months have passed since last she saw him and then he is there, stepping into the tiny room, this man with the face of a stone gargoyle, sunken black eyes, deep cheeks, sharp cheekbones, all brutality and shame. Yakha stands with her dry lips. Her daughter, the little girl in a faded sweatshirt that matches the blue-green antibiotic paste on her mysterious sores—she leans into her mother and cries, eyes squeezed shut, her hands tight around a blonde doll. Yakha strokes her daughter's hair and tucks it behind one ear. Gentle, her hand. Everyone standing stunned.

He is taking them back to Chechnya. That is that. They are going back to Grozny.

And what does Ruslan make of all of this? Because, yes, Ruslan is there, too. Yakha knows him from his first days in Ingushetia, when he and his mother slept on the floor of the train station bathroom. Yakha was there; she and Ruslan's mother found each other, two women without husbands, pariahs among the exiles, Ruslan's mother fading into her unknowable pains and her vodka.

Ruslan calls them his family. Yakha is up at 4:30 a.m. every morning to wash her face and do the laundry at the station before it's time to wake the children—six of them, from age four to seventeen—and feed them tomatoes, cucumbers, buckwheat if she has it. The oldest brother is Borz, who sits on the torn and stained easy chair beside the TV that was a gift but never worked, wearing track pants and the faraway look of the sitting-room gurus of a thousand teenage generations. Sometimes, Ruslan lies across his new brother's arm and listens to stories about, for example, the time Borz ran away from his father. When his father caught him, he chained his feet and shackled him to the wall; he was given food once a day, which he ate standing up because he was only allowed to lie down at night. It was Borz who showed Ruslan how to clean his teeth by wiping them on his shirt. Last Friday, they gave him a blue backpack. Yes, they are a family.

And no, Yakha would not be returning to Chechnya. She was not going back to the war. ✢

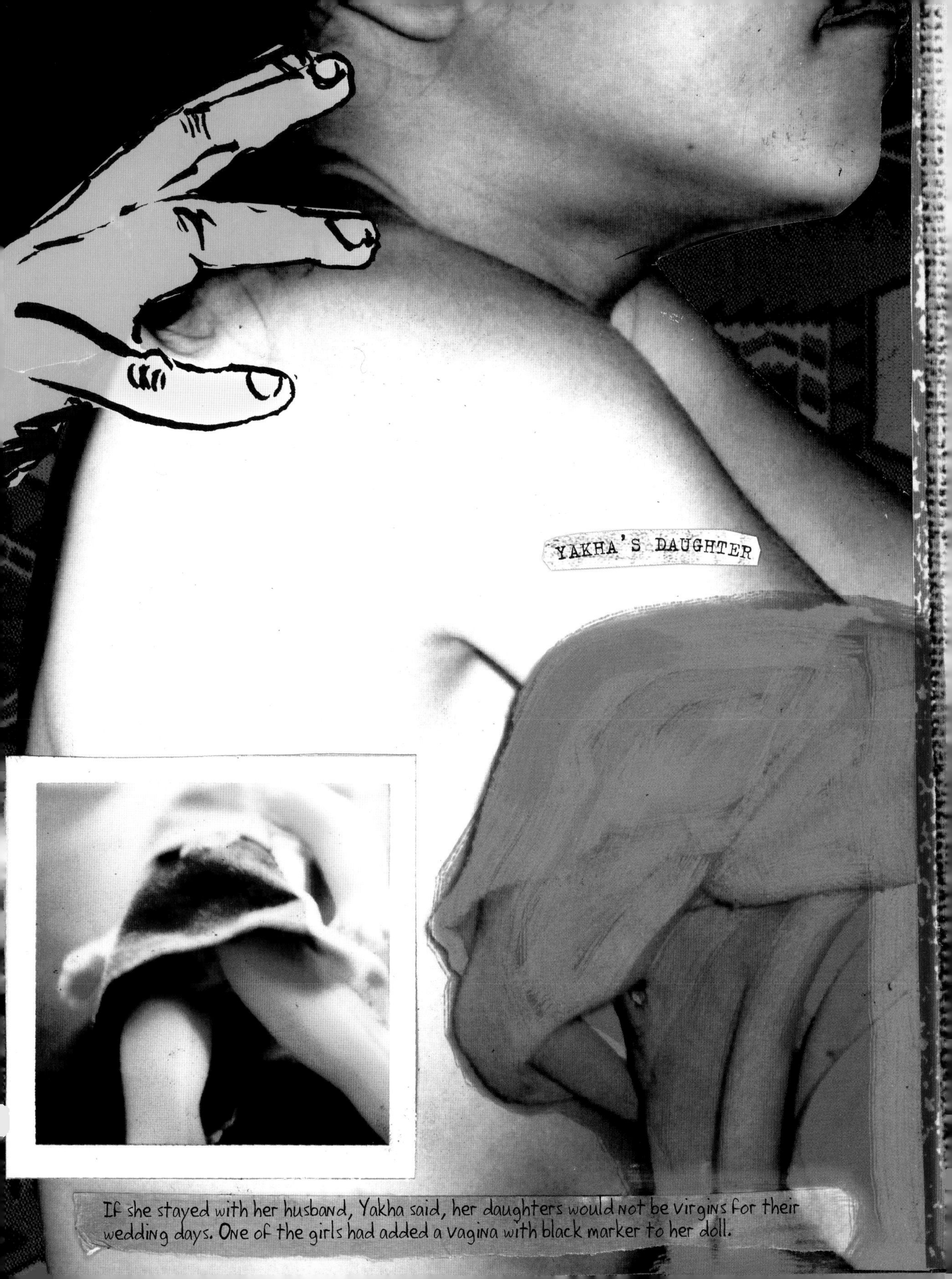
YAKHA'S DAUGHTER

If she stayed with her husband, Yakha said, her daughters would not be virgins for their wedding days. One of the girls had added a vagina with black marker to her doll.

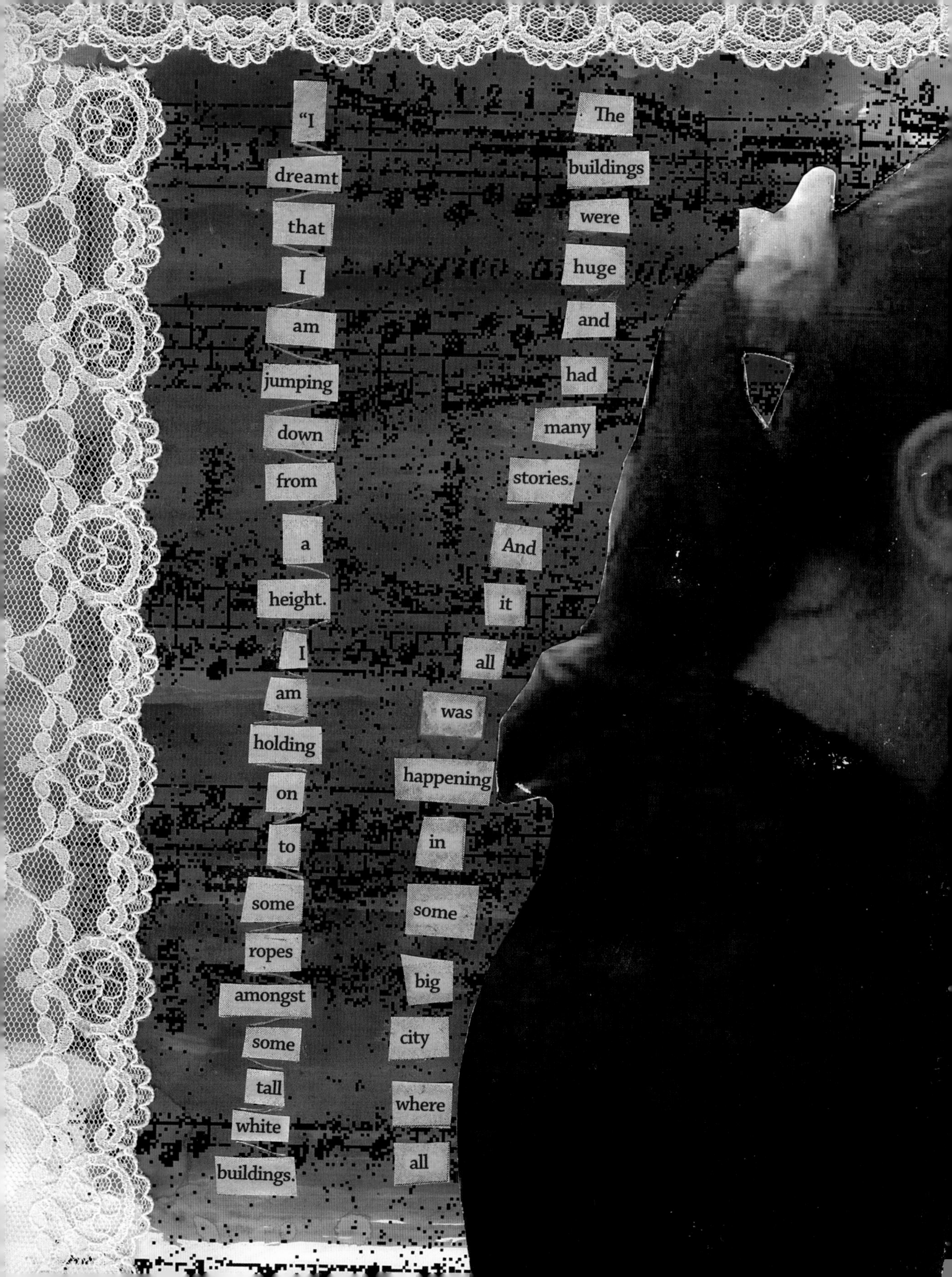
"I dreamt that I am jumping down from a height. I am holding on to some ropes amongst some tall white buildings.
The buildings were huge and had many stories. And it all was happening in some big city some where all

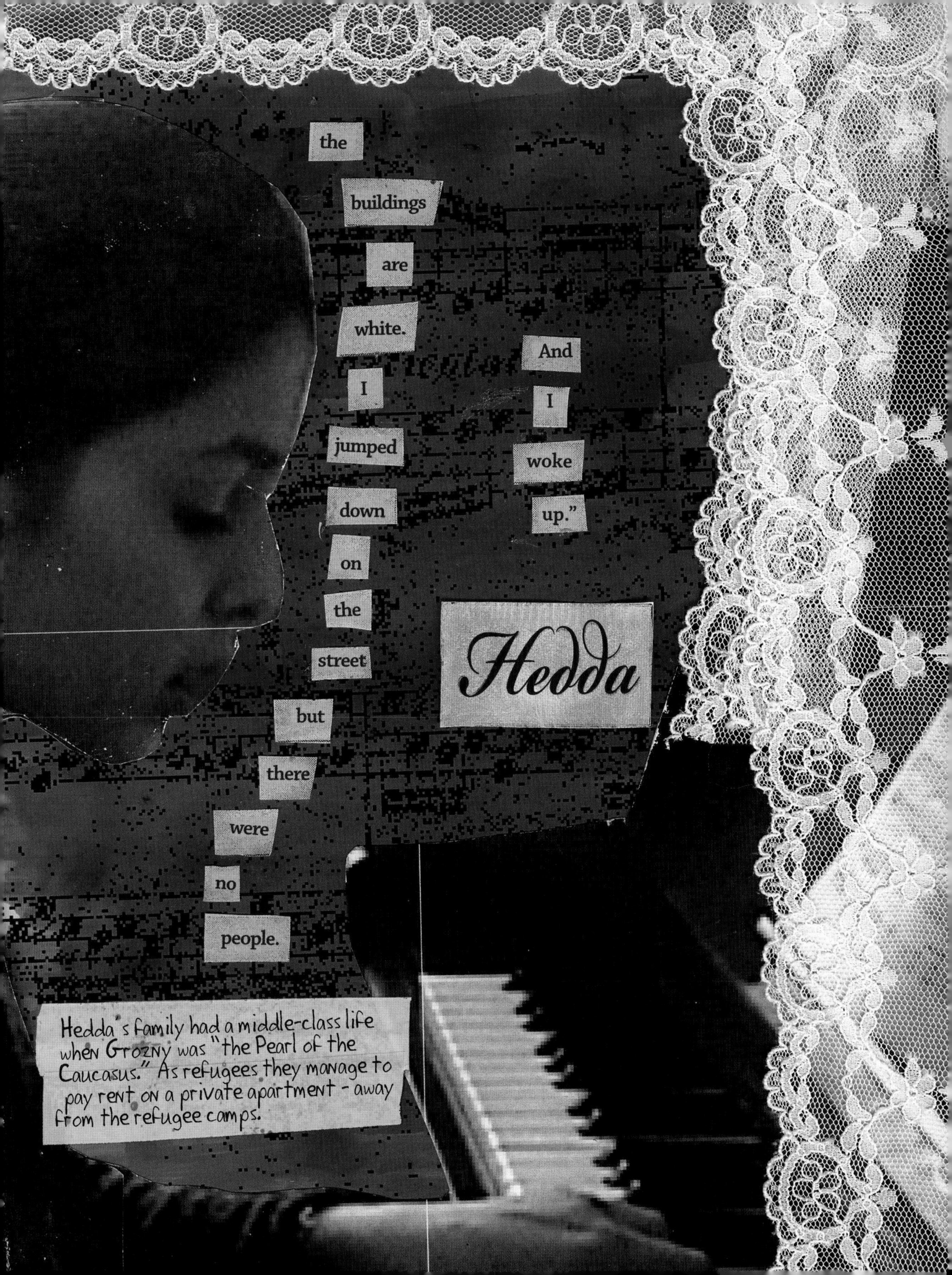
the buildings are white. I jumped down on the street but there were no people.
And I woke up."
Hedda
Hedda's family had a middle-class life when Grozny was "the Pearl of the Caucasus." As refugees they manage to pay rent on a private apartment - away from the refugee camps.

he cement pathway is cracked with age, its surface buckled by weeds. There are no trees around here, though there are a few tired bushes. This is a planned residential area. The path leads to a low-rise apartment building; its concrete, once white, has grayed with age and begun to yellow. The silence here is as striking as the sun, which is too bright—a hard light that dulls the patchy grass, blunts the outline of the building, and mutes the day. The building is dwarfed by its neighbors, taller versions of itself that recede for perhaps half a kilometer, growing whiter and whiter with distance. The uniformity induces a slight sense of disorientation—this place could be almost anywhere, this could be any time within the past sixty years. It's like a silent dream; you are caught in a place with no center, no history. As though a bomb had fallen and left only the buildings intact, empty of life, of memory, of stories: anonymous.

In reality, this building is very specific, rooted in history: It is a Soviet-era apartment building. There are millions of them all across the former Soviet Union, many tall, some squat; all started out white. There is never just one, there is always a complex. This makes it difficult to tell, in isolation, where any given building might be situated. But an aerial view of this residential complex places it in a low-lying area of the small, mountainous republic named Ingushetia, which borders a likewise small, mountainous republic named Chechnya. The ruins of clan castles, fortifications, and watchtowers dot the Caucasian peaks, and sheep pour through the mountain passes in spring.

Identical windows at regular intervals reflect the glare of the sun, some painfully with their tinfoil covering, others more gently thanks to pale curtains. From a top-floor window, an aloe plant peeks out from behind nylon lace. The base of the building is hemmed only with dried mud, a result of rain splashing up from the earth. There are no hardy geraniums or mums or tough shrubs anywhere; they were not part of the plan.

The mesh-reinforced glass door opens directly onto the ground floor, suddenly dark and cool. It takes a moment for the eyes to adjust; the overhead bulb is not lit. Two people start up the concrete stairs. One looks younger than her years, the other more weathered. They are the woman from the West, and her translator.

Their footsteps sound hollow as they mount the four flights and step out onto the top floor. Only now does it strike the visitors that the most distinctive feature of this building is its silence. The translator knocks at the wooden door—it is surprisingly hard on the knuckles. The wood grain turns out to be the kind that comes in stick-on rolls—the door is actually metal. It is opened by a round, middle-aged woman. She smiles and her dark brown eyes glisten. She extends a soft hand and squeezes the visitors' hands in turn with a warmth and strength that feels more like an embrace than a handshake. She speaks and the translator translates: "Welcome."

The visitors step into the one-bedroom apartment and remove their shoes, adding them to a mat crowded with the shoes of this family of eight. The family must have brought the furnishings with them when they fled Grozny; there isn't much, but it is a visual feast after the rest of the building. A maroon rug hangs on the wall; more rugs, richly dyed in greens and golds, cover the floor, the effect at once Celtic and Islamic. On one wall is a framed photo of a handsome man in his thirties. Bearded, unsmiling but warm, he has the same splendid coffee-dark eyes as the mother of the house. In one chair, an impossibly old-looking little man sits wrinkled and rosy. He is the grandfather. In a corner of the couch, a tiny but frail elderly woman, her skin like parchment, eyes distant and vague, sits wrapped in a rustic woolen scarf despite the heat of the apartment; she is mumbling—praying? The father of the family rises and welcomes the visitors. He's balding, with a comfortable, bookish look, decently dressed but a little rumpled.

He offers them coffee. No, he was not a professor, he was an executive at the Grozny Oil Institute. The institute is gone, the oil turned to a slick on the water and smoke in the air.

The coffee smells rich, dark and articulate, overpowering the other aromas of fresh cheese, smoked fish, cooked eggs. Good smells, homey smells, but crowded into too small a space, they seem a slight embarrassment to the mother of the house, who opens the kitchen window. As she does so, she brushes aside the nylon curtain and the visitors glimpse the aloe plant on the sill.

There are three little girls. All under age nine, they nonetheless appear to be mini-women. There is a gravitas in their eyes, despite the doll clutched by the eldest; gravitas even in the eyes of the youngest. There are not enough chairs for all of them to sit, but they lean, one curving herself against the arm of her father's chair, the other resting against her grandfather's shoulder, the middle one snuggled next to her grandmother, who appears not to register her presence. From their vantage points they examine the visitors, especially the woman; her long shiny dark hair, her clothes, her graceful gestures. She is from a place where streets are not punctuated by craters; where people don't live in basements open to the sky; where soldiers don't come in the middle of the night. Where your mother and father don't wake you before dawn one day and say, "Shhh, my darling. Come, we're leaving."

Hedda.

She enters the room reluctantly, ahead of her mother who gently ushers her in. She is fifteen. Too pale. Her fair hair is pulled back into a ponytail. Her eyes, light blue and downcast beneath a fan of minklike lashes. At her temples lie a tracing of veins. Her mouth is sensitive, serious. Her mother exits briefly and returns with a piano bench. Hedda sits, obedient. It is evident she is pretty but her prettiness is in abeyance, like an unlit chandelier in a disused room.

She does not make eye contact. She answers questions briefly, each word seeming to tug down the corners of her mouth as though painfully extracted. She hugs herself and is still at first, but soon begins to shift, twisting slightly in place, head tilted, her gaze moving across the floor.

"Who is your favorite composer?"

"Beethoven."

"Why is that, Hedda?"

Her reply is inaudible. The translator asks her to repeat herself. She does. The translator pauses, glances apologetically at the woman visitor who says, "That's okay—," quick to let Hedda off the hook, but Hedda says something else and the translator pauses once more, then says, "It's difficult to express this, um . . . She says she likes Beethoven because he—that is, through his music, she is able to connect to her own . . . darkness."

The mother brings in a tray of coffee and sweets. The sweets are homemade and a very special treat. The little girls wait for the guests and their elders to help themselves, then pounce as politely as possible. The middle one places a morsel between her grandmother's lips. Honey cake and almond cookies.

The youngest daughter asks Hedda something, Hedda nods imperceptibly, and the child helps herself to another portion. Her sisters immediately lay claim to a share of it amid a shy burst of chatter directed at the woman visitor. The translator explains: "They are having Hedda's share. Hedda doesn't eat with the family. She prefers to eat alone."

"Why?"

Hedda squints briefly and shifts her gaze intently up at an angle. The woman visitor allows her own gaze to follow Hedda's to the corner of the ceiling. What is written there?

The woman asks, "Are you able to take music lessons in Ingushetia?"

Hedda nods yes. Pauses, adds something.

"Yes," says the translator, "but she can't compete the way she did in Grozny."

Hedda, still looking up, confides something else to the corner of the ceiling.

"She says she wants to go back home to Grozny."

"Grozny," says the grandfather sharply.

The woman turns to him; his eyes are on her, bright with good humor, in contrast with his tone. She holds his gaze while the translator says, "He wants to know if you know what Grozny was called before the war."

The woman shakes her head.

The grandfather leans forward and confides a brief reply.

The translator: "The Pearl of the Caucasus."

Perhaps that ceiling corner serves Hedda as a tabula rasa. A blank screen where she can rest her thoughts. They flicker, syncopated shades of black and white like musical notes that have flown free of the bars of the staff. They're safe up there. Nesting. Waiting to fly back to her, to reassume their places, their beautiful order. Order and beauty equal art and art equals freedom. But for now let them rest and flutter, groom themselves and chatter.

The translator continues, "There weren't supposed to be Russian soldiers here in Ingushetia, at least not doing the same job—"

"*Zachistka*," says the grandfather.

"Cleanup raids." The grandfather is speaking quickly now in his rasping voice, and the translator interprets with some difficulty, "'Why have we been followed here? The answer: The Russian soldiers are here to convince us all that it is safe to go home again. Our neighbors here in our host country are called our 'cousins.' We are almost the same people but there is a border that separates our countries and that border was supposed to keep us safe from the soldiers once we left home but they came anyway. And now our 'cousins' want us to go home too."

Now the father speaks in his more measured way, and the adults of the family, with the exception of the grandmother, burst out laughing. The translator smiles and says, "When you are visiting relatives it is important not to overstay your welcome."

The eldest of the little girls pipes up. The other two pipe up. They all talk at once.

The translator gets a word in. "When they get back to Grozny, they are going to look for their . . . it's a little chocolate bear." He smiles and shrugs. The little girls laugh, and the youngest one jumps up and down in place.

"The chocolate bear was hidden by their uncle." Now the little girls point enthusiastically at the photo of the handsome man for the benefit of the woman visitor, who does her best to follow the translator's account amid their frequent delighted interruptions.

"He—their uncle—has hidden several chocolate bears in their house in Grozny, and they found them, one for each girl, and even Hedda ate hers with the rest of them, but their uncle said there was one more that he hid for good luck. Well, they couldn't find that one and it's still there and he said he would tell them where it was next time he came."

The squeals and interjections die down, then Hedda speaks quietly to the floor. The little girls, their eyes still on the woman, nod in sage agreement with their older sister.

"Their house is gone," says the translator, "but it doesn't mean that the bear is gone too. Sometimes a whole house is bombed but one teacup survives. In Grozny, Hedda has seen a whole kitchen—a kitchen suite, you know the table and chairs—sitting outside among the bricks and glass, perfectly intact."

There is a silence. The mother pours more coffee into the visitors' cups. After a moment, Hedda's mother addresses her and Hedda rises and leaves the room. The mother turns to her guests, picks up the piano bench and, gesturing for them to follow, says in English, "Please."

The piano is afforded a privacy unavailable to the rest of the family. An upright, freshly polished with orange oil, adorned with a length of white lace, it resides on the other side of the small entrance vestibule in a space that is less than a room but more than a closet.

Sheet music is stacked in neat piles on the piano and the floor. Piece after piece is arranged according to invisible criteria. Why is "Liebestraum" in the same pile as the Bartók piece? Classical pieces, romantic pieces, baroque pieces, French pieces, Russian pieces; pieces and pieces and pieces. Bach and Beethoven are open on the piano side by side as though Hedda had started playing page one of "Preludio II" and continued straight into the twenty-fourth bar of the "Moonlight" Sonata.

Hedda plays.

I want to go home. I make a path with my eyes to and from school. I make a corridor of what I see and I stay inside it. This is so that I will stay ready to go home. I keep my eyes on the ground about twenty feet ahead. In this way I follow the same path even if my feet are carrying me in a new direction. Keep to the path. If you get into the habit of looking around and swinging your arms or even letting your facial expression change too easily by smiling; if you allow your words or any of your sounds, like laughter, to go off in any old direction into the air, pieces of you can get lost and you'll never find them again when it's time to go home.

"Preludio II" has begun in midargument. Lucid, vigorous.

Those pieces will fly around like bits of paper, unable to find each other. Like letters of the alphabet or musical notes, they don't mean anything on their own; they are not a word *or a* sentence *or a* story *or a* chord *or a* melody *or a* mood *or a* symphony—

Gathering speed against taut reins, adamant, almost angry, but always in control.

Most of the time I don't chat. I don't mind if other people do. But thoughts and feelings and words go off all warm and alive into the air and they never come back. They get lost. They are especially apt to do this when people are eating.

A fleeting, plaintive note, caught and held resolutely in check. The piece slows, reasserts its dignity, its reason; the point it was making—points, rather, for this argument has many sides—

The notes fly off in all directions and get lost. Farther and farther from home; flying and flying until its heart beats out. Home is music. Without home, the notes are just sounds.

The "Moonlight" Sonata.

I know our house is gone, our street is gone. They've gone to pieces and pieces and pieces. If I were older, I'd go back and start putting them back together again. That's what a lot of the mothers are doing right now, with their bare hands. They've already put the train station back together again.

She is beautiful when she plays. Her face lit and shadowed by turns as though clouds were passing rapidly overhead. She is awake.

Everything is somewhere. Science tells us that. It's called the Law of Conservation of Mass. It is impossible for anything in the universe to just go away. It might turn into something else, or it might be smashed, but its ingredients are still there, and doesn't

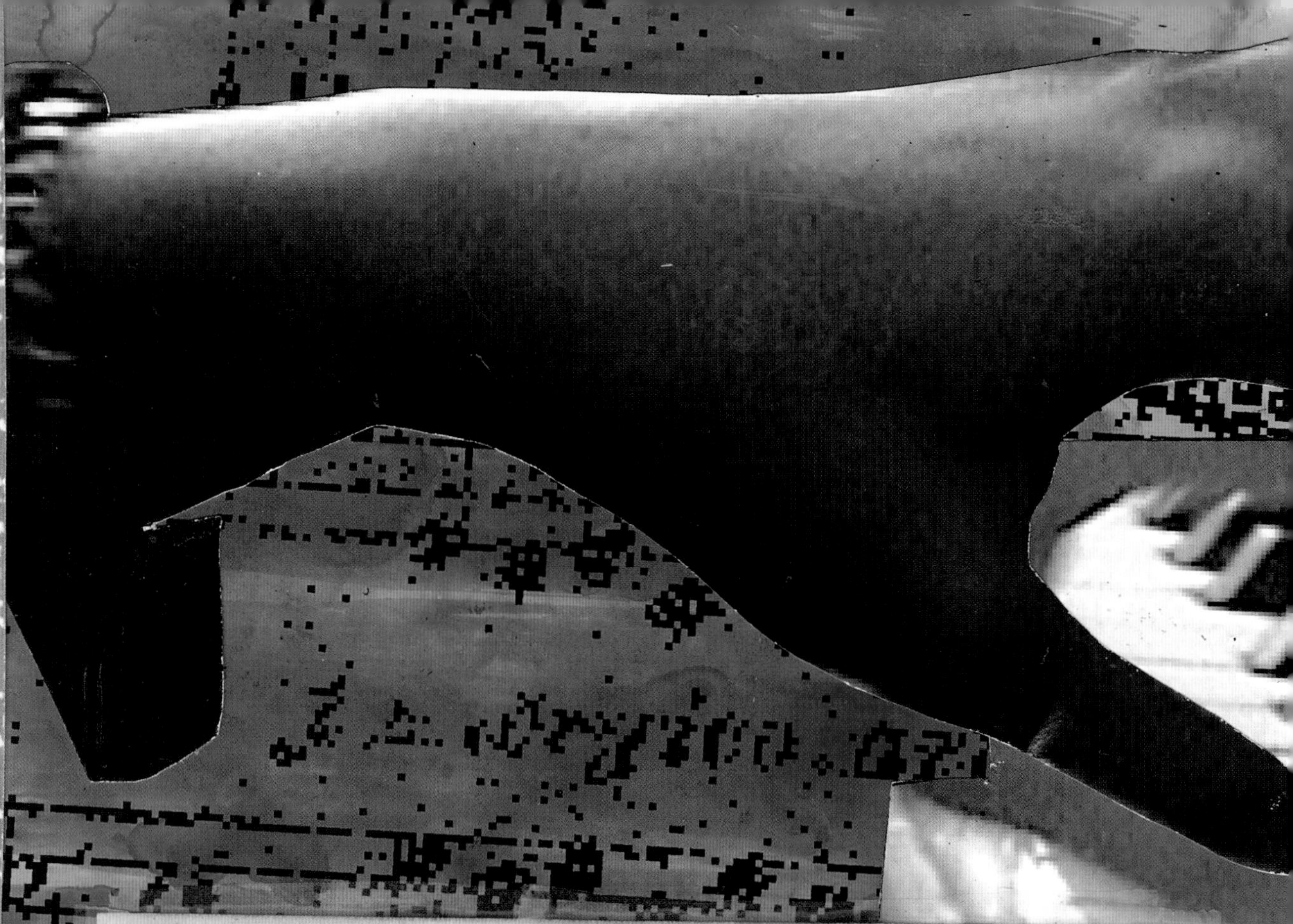

that mean that it is possible, at least in theory, to put anything back together again? Dishes, photographs, even chocolate bears in tinfoil.

Her mouth works, lower lip passing between her teeth; she rocks slowly, as though pushing a beloved weight. The music is a lament, a love song to the night, plush and dark like the maroon rug hanging on the wall. Hedda is engaged in an intimate conversation with the notes. She leans into them, gathering memory and emotion and some untold story that is far beyond her years, far outside her experience, even her era; playing like a heroine in an old Russian novel.

Sounds can hurt you. They are solid. The bombs come screaming, grinning, obscene. Those sounds are an abomination. Someone should pray for those sounds. They are trapped in hell.

Is Hedda like this because she is a refugee? Because she is a virtuoso? Because she is an adolescent? Would she be pale, careful, nonverbal, in a Canadian suburb? Would she be as gifted without the bombs? Or would she thrive in her peculiar way just about anywhere, like the aloe on the windowsill? Braving the blight of peace and privilege to insist upon the darkness of the piano room on sunny days when other kids are enjoying "the best years of their lives."

Silence is not the opposite of sound. Silence that is unpunctuated by sound is meaningless, just as sound unpunctuated by silence is meaningless. Both are noise. Both are exiled from meaning. They have no center, no pattern. No identity. Anonymous.

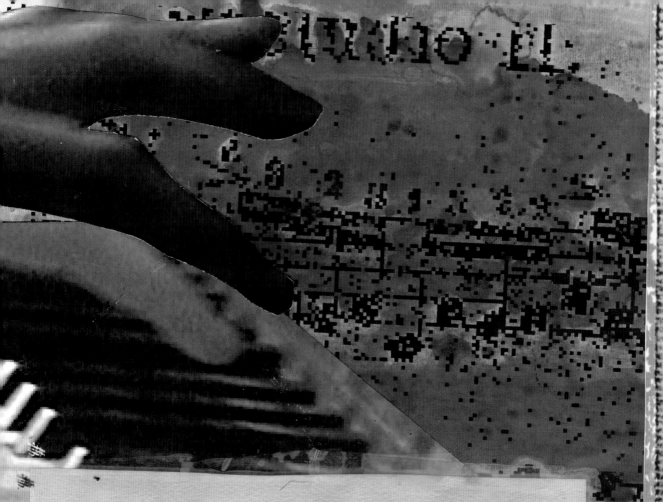

The bars of the staff are a ladder, a latticework to support life, a frame upon which to weave a fabric. A rope upon which you can swing to safety even if all around you is white and silent and stillborn.

She finishes playing. Straightens. Her features begin to compose themselves once more, preparing to resume their sleepwalking life, but her mouth is still soft, eyes wide. She looks at the woman visitor who has been leaning, motionless against the wall, and speaks. The translator, crouched in the small doorway, rises and all but whispers Hedda's words to the woman.

"Her uncle is dead. He was assassinated. They think it happened in the mountains outside Grozny."

"I'm so sorry. Tell her I'm so sorry."

Hedda shakes her head, still looking down, and grimaces. She is crying, then just as quickly has stopped. She looks up, directly into the woman's eyes and speaks in a level tone.

"She says she's going to stop talking now."

Hedda leaves the alcove that houses the piano. The woman says, "Thank you, Hedda."

At the door, the woman and her translator put their shoes back on. Hedda reappears between her parents. She hands the woman a single piece of sheet music.

Outside, the sun is brilliant to the point of belligerence. The visitors shade their eyes; behind them the apartment buildings recede, bleached. They walk toward their car. The woman visitor sits in the relative shade and looks down at the piece of music that Hedda has given her, and reads between the bars:

"I dreamt that I am jumping down from a height. I am holding on to some ropes amongst some tall white buildings...." ✛

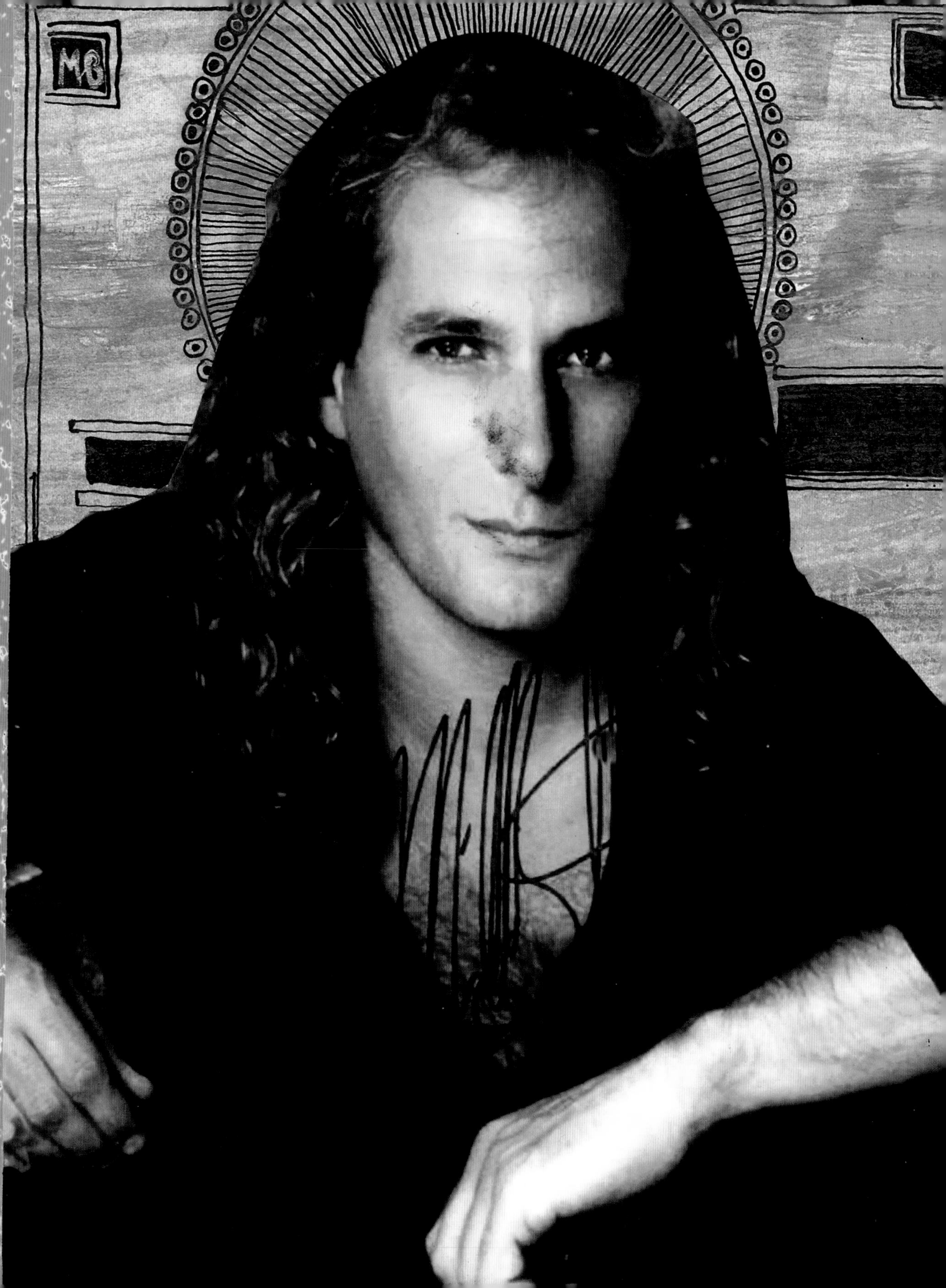
MB

✳ ✳ ✳ ✳ ✳ NAZRAN. THE HOTEL ASSA. ✳ ✳ ✳ ✳ ✳

He walked - or rather swaggered - into the hotel restaurant, his camera slung over his shoulder like an ax. He was the Michael Bolton of war photographers.

MB, my name for the Dane, somehow turned the breakfast room into a high school cafeteria. He was the cool kid in grade seven who smoked pot, got straight As, and came from a family that had a bread-maker.

It was my fourth day in Ingushetia. The war correspondents had arrived.

MB tossed his blond mane and straddled his chair. His camera clattered on the table as if to announce that he had arrived from his ice-capped mountain.

I met him that evening. I sat at a table with the visiting journalists, all of whom had reported wars all over the world. One, just back from Liberia, described the National Patriotic Front guerrillas, dressed like trannies as they rode through the streets of Monrovia, spitting machine-gun bullets into the air. Another described savage nights in the Congo, far from family, safety, and food, hiding in dirt huts as rebels pillaged and burned villages. Yet another described civil-war refugee camps in Sudan, cut off from all aid, where children died in his arms, bellies popping with malnutrition.

Finally, MB looked up from his food. He pulled his T-shirt down so we could all see his neck. There were faint red scars. He had been stationed in Hebron, he said, photographing young Palestinian militants throwing Molotov cocktails at Israeli soldiers. Then the soldiers opened fire.

I sat silently, listening. I scraped my Converse sneakers against the linoleum. What story could I tell the war correspondents? I could see that they were puzzled as to why I was in Ingushetia. Should I begin with the fact that my whole family is terrified of water? My grandparents wanted their family on dry land, and close. So close that both my aunts have lived only miles away from my grandmother for most of their lives. They see each other every day.

My father's parents left Germany on a boat, all of their secrets, grief, and rage hidden like sea stars in the ocean that they crossed. When they arrived in Nova Scotia, they were advised to change my father's name from Severin to Sheldon, to assimilate into their new home. Did this help? When my father changed his name, did my grandmother feel as if she'd lost another child? Now my father likes to travel; they never want him to leave. Hysteria accompanies his departures, my father repeating his itinerary over and over again to my grandfather. As a child, we were always at my grandparents' house for our Friday night Shabbat dinner. Hazy from stolen gulps of Manischewitz, I would watch my grandfather vanish. His eyes dark slits, mouth open in mute horror. Sometimes, he would stop talking for days.

Now I see this in my own father. These silences like flotsam. My father stockpiles tins of food in his cupboards. "Just in case," he says. My grandfather watches us carefully, like an assembly-line foreman, to make sure we never waste food. We should never waste. We should savor crumbs like we should savor touch. Sometimes, my grandfather would put my father's articles in an old plastic grocery bag and walk for miles to show a friend what his son had written. His son had accomplished something. His son was a track star. His son was going overseas to study in London. And his daughter? His daughter was a nurse. His daughter was a beauty queen, Miss Côte Saint-Luc. Accomplishment was the certain victory over those who had tried to execute him and his family.

I won't ask them about Izhou, though. If I do, my grandfather will start walking in circles. My grandmother will start to make lemon tea and just say my name over and over again. It must have been only a matter of seconds. My grandmother's hand separated from his, and then Izhou was gone.

This is what I know: Izhou, you were born in Lodz, Poland. You played the violin. In 1944, the Lodz Ghetto was liquidated. By then, rumors must have reached Lodz that mass exterminations were taking place. Did my grandmother know where the two of you were going? And when the Nazis put her in one line and you in another, did she know what would happen next?

We are not a family of swimmers. Anyone who swims might drown and never come back. My mother tried so hard to get me to swim, to break this family compulsion. Private lessons at the community center, white sand holiday beaches. I would wade in up to my ankles, holding my breath, squeezing my eyes shut.

My mother was afraid of the winter - afraid of falling. She fell once when she was eight months pregnant with my sister. After that, she walked as little as possible. Her purple shearling boots sat in our hallway, their waves of salt stains a reminder of her terrifying battle from her car to her classroom each day.

The winter was not the only thing in Canada that made her feel like a foreign body. It was the little things - like when she first arrived in Canada, she would put the vegetable peels in the kitchen sink in a plastic bag just like her mother, Reni, had done for its convenience. My aunt pulled her aside. "We don't do that here. It's dirty. We put garbage in the can <u>right away</u>." The house where my mother grew up was a salon of languages: French, Hebrew, and Bulgarian; visitors who brought Turkish coffee, bourekas, olives, conversation. Here in Canada, it was so often quiet. Joy replaced the blankness when an aerogram would arrive. The letters smelled of Reni's perfume - Opium - and her tobacco. My mother read them over and over, as though each word were a small boat taking her back across the sea to her parents' home in Jaffa. As a child, I often wondered if my mother would leave us for her old home, like she had done when she was six. Her family had come to Israel from Bulgaria after the war. Unnoticed by her parents, my mother packed a small bag and left the house. She walked to Jaffa's beach and followed the shoreline in the hope that it would eventually take her back home.

Once, as an adult, in Tulum, Mexico, a friend pleaded with me to come into the ocean. He was a swimmer who couldn't understand why I never wanted to go near the water. I asked him to hold my hand as he pulled me out to sea. Salty waves began to lap over my head. I buried my head in his chest as he swam farther and farther from the shore. Then he let go of my hand. And I began to swim, catching my breath, holding my head above water, my first time doing this alone. Squinting in the sun in this warm turquoise sea.

All the war correspondents seemed disappointed by Ingushetia. They must have come expecting the images of bombed, electrocuted Grozny. Little Chechen boys, dark and haunted, hiding in basements as the bombs fell.

And what is there, here in Ingushetia?

Children who swarm the journalists like butterflies on flowers. Chechen women with flour on their hands. Photos, rings, dolls, furled letters, pillows, broken cassette tapes. There is a lot of quiet. Or rather, a sort of melancholy din. No explosions; no women strapping bombs to their bellies and blowing up markets.

The story was in Grozny, the journalists said. Yes, the story must be in Grozny. They had arranged visas, and the FSB, the federal security service of the Russian Federation, would accompany them to Grozny tomorrow.

ZARIMA

"My name is Zarima Koloyeva. I have been in bed all day.

In 1997 my father died. I have finished two grades of school. I became sick and failed to continue.

My hands swell up in the cold. My father also had this.

I have not left this room in one year. When we first arrived at Tanzila, I played outside with the kids for three months. I don't want to go outside anymore because I'm angry. And that is really all I want to say."

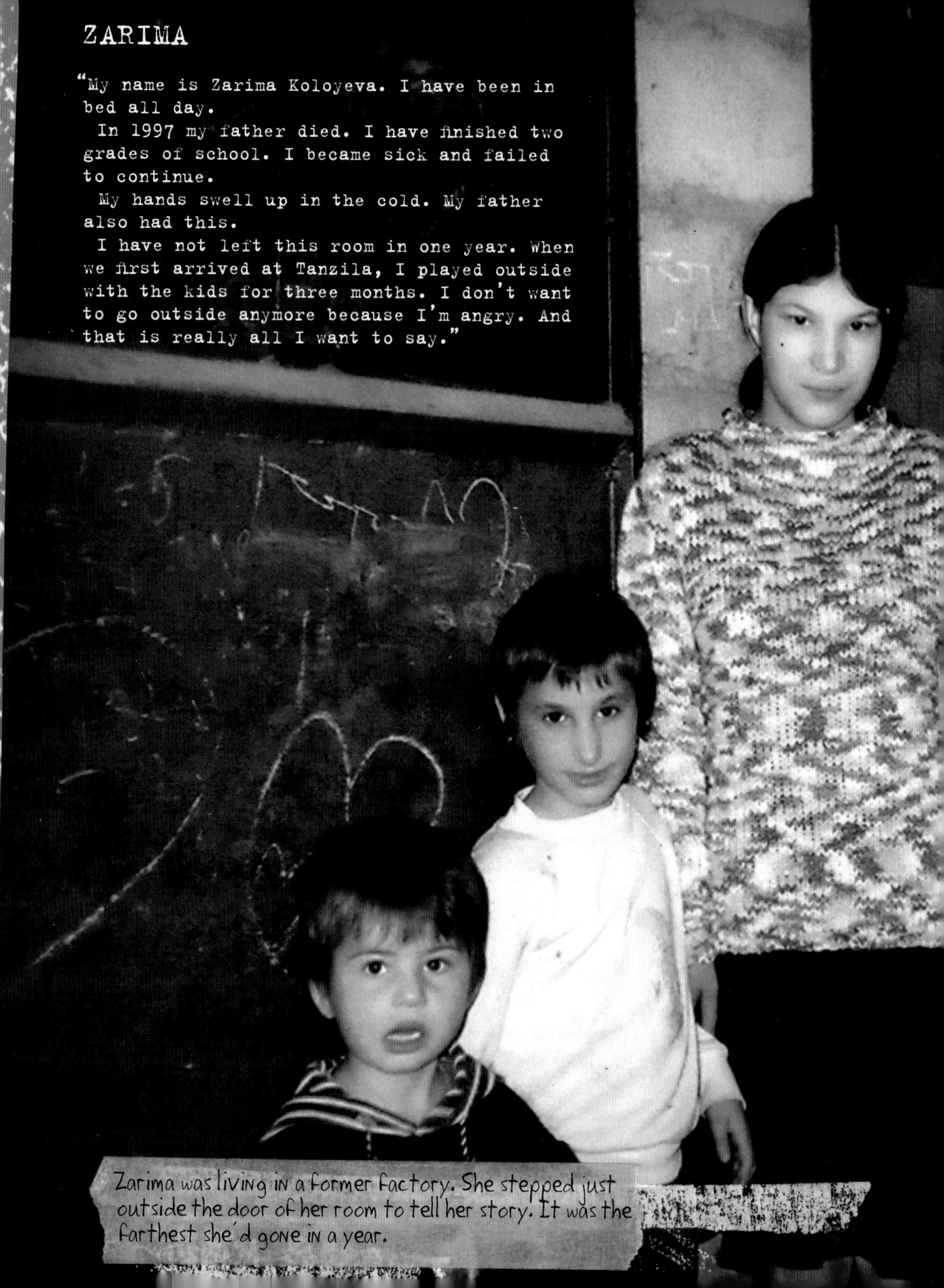

Zarima was living in a former factory. She stepped just outside the door of her room to tell her story. It was the farthest she'd gone in a year.

ZALINA

"This is Zalina. She lives in the camp. She sleeps in this room, with me.

Zalina likes to be outside the room. She plays with other girls. She likes to play hide-and-go-seek. She loves Diana Gurtskaya, the famous singer. Zalina loves pie and cake. Her favorite film is called Wild Angel.

She has a lot of friends. She has been in the camp a very long time. She likes to be outside."

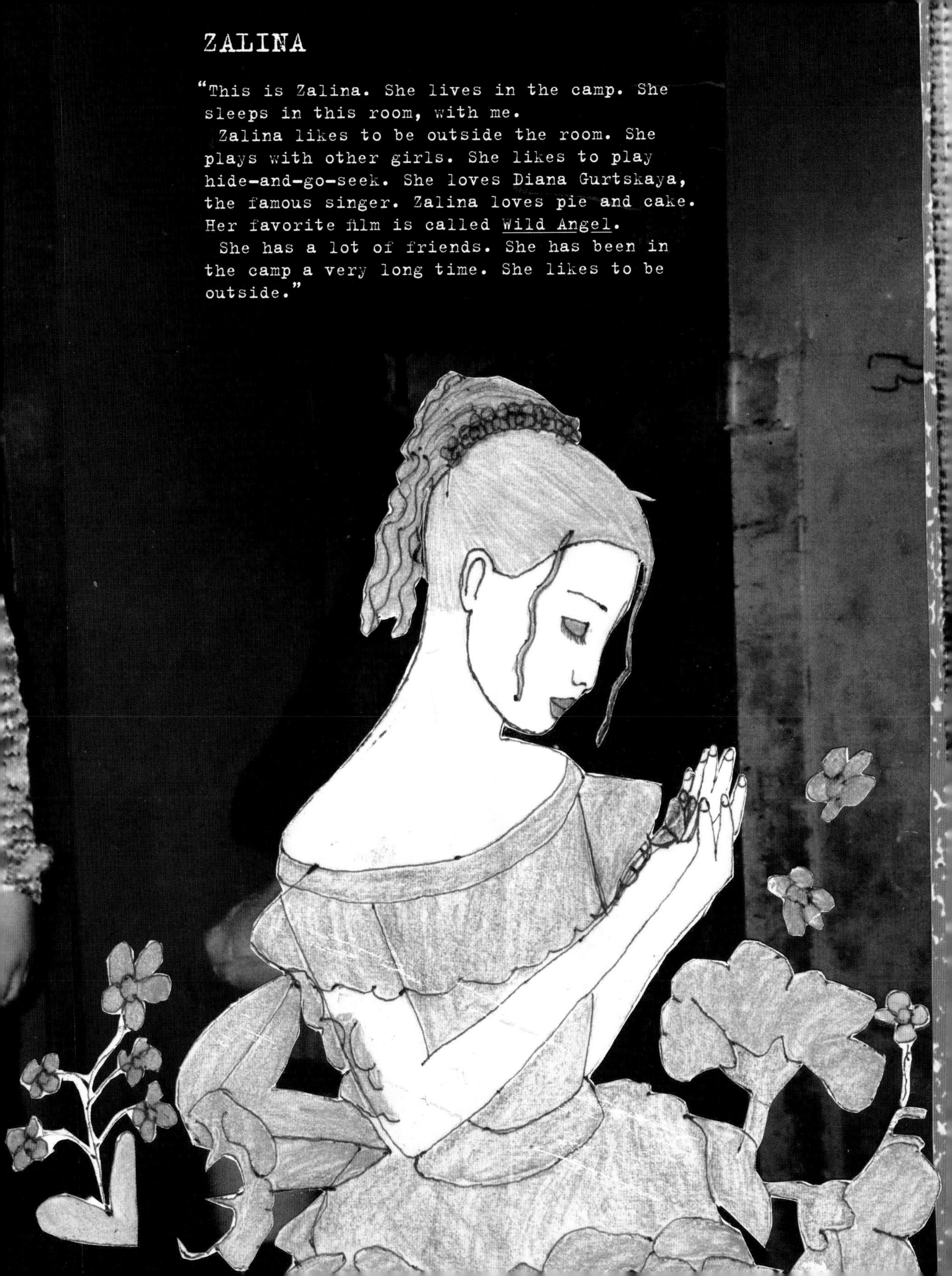

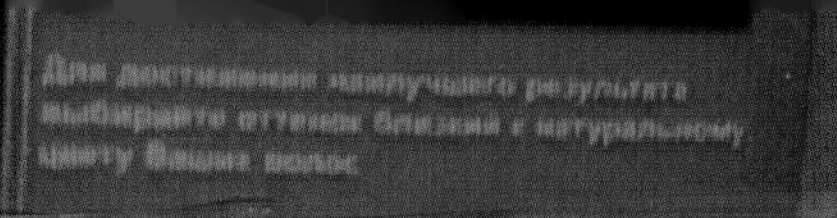
Для достижения наилучшего результата выбирайте оттенки близкие к натуральному цвету Ваших волос

3. THE DAYCARE LADY

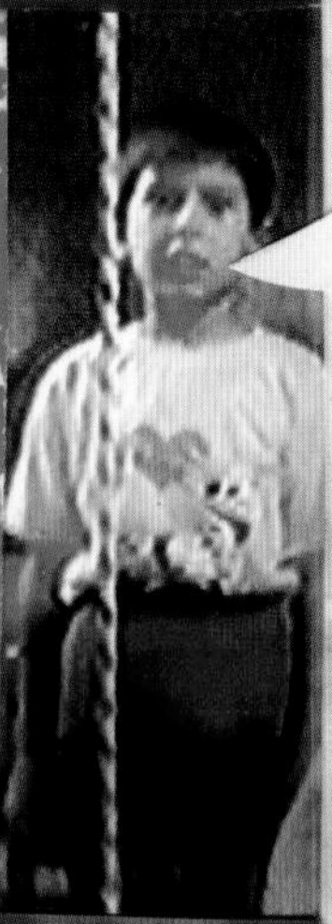

My friends, if one of you's
a martyr
to love and suffers
hopelessly,
you'll live a wretched life,
it's true,
you will live, though, you
may be sure

This is how the day really begins. Not with stooping to pick up the trash that the wind leaves every night on the porch, and not with the squeak of the galvanized bucket as her son fetches water, but with this, a few lines from Aleksandr Pushkin. Her son reads, and she follows the words into daydreams. *Ruslan and Ludmila*. How many Ruslans are there in Tanzila camp? Too many. But it's a popular name.

She puts on her foundation, Max Factor, the one with the sunscreen, and while it dries she makes her bed. She is "the Daycare Lady," but is that how she feels? One doesn't have to feel like a person who shares seven backed-up toilets and a single working shower with 1,167 other people, all of them shitting now in buckets and washing in buckets as well. And how many more people might arrive today?

She puts her powder on, pancake makeup from the market. How does she feel? How does she actually feel? Today she has chosen a high-waisted red skirt, the same red as the plastic washbasins, and a tailored, crushed-velvet top, patterned and golden. The skirt has slits to just above the knee, and the top is sleeveless.

She does her eyes, Momtaz-brand pencil and liquid liner, plus Max Factor mascara. She applies the wand only to the center of the lashes; she has found that this makes her eyes seem larger.

The camp was once just a café, the Tanzila Café. One day, the first refugee moved in. Now there's a school, a daycare, two clinics, four little stores, a games room, a billiard hall, and still who knows how many refugees crowded in above the café. The rest live in rooms in the abandoned factories, or in railcars, or tents, or an assortment of shacks and sheds. The international aid workers who fly in from cities where men and women sit at sidewalk tables stirring chocolate into their coffee—they like to try out their jargon. They call it the "Tanzila temporary settlement." They call the people "internally displaced persons," but they are given their correction: We are not misplaced Russians. We are Chechen refugees.

Waterproof lip liner, Claudio brand, from Germany. Jane Ashley lipstick. These will smooth the cleft of her upper lip. The overall effect is businesslike, but at the same time expectant. One does not have to feel like a refugee.

Another family is moving into the camp, but the Daycare Lady doesn't know this and she doesn't need to know, because every time it is the same and yet unique to the smallest detail. In this case, it will be six children and a soft mother who wears no makeup and covers her hair with a flowered kerchief, and who isn't even moving into the camp on account of the war, exactly, but rather because her husband has appeared out of nowhere and her husband is the war. So: another woman with no husband in the camp. The Tanzila ladies will have a few things to say about that! She's not an "internally displaced person." She's a refugee.

Six more children for the school and the daycare. One is bound to be named Ruslan. Three are boys,

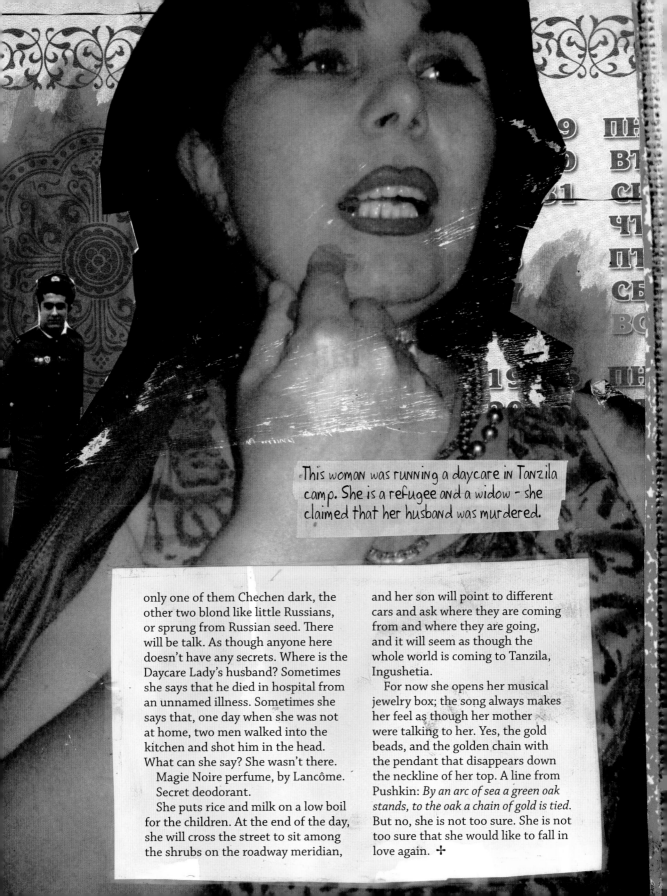

This woman was running a daycare in Tanzila camp. She is a refugee and a widow – she claimed that her husband was murdered.

only one of them Chechen dark, the other two blond like little Russians, or sprung from Russian seed. There will be talk. As though anyone here doesn't have any secrets. Where is the Daycare Lady's husband? Sometimes she says that he died in hospital from an unnamed illness. Sometimes she says that, one day when she was not at home, two men walked into the kitchen and shot him in the head. What can she say? She wasn't there.

Magie Noire perfume, by Lancôme. Secret deodorant.

She puts rice and milk on a low boil for the children. At the end of the day, she will cross the street to sit among the shrubs on the roadway meridian, and her son will point to different cars and ask where they are coming from and where they are going, and it will seem as though the whole world is coming to Tanzila, Ingushetia.

For now she opens her musical jewelry box; the song always makes her feel as though her mother were talking to her. Yes, the gold beads, and the golden chain with the pendant that disappears down the neckline of her top. A line from Pushkin: *By an arc of sea a green oak stands, to the oak a chain of gold is tied.* But no, she is not too sure. She is not too sure that she would like to fall in love again. ✛

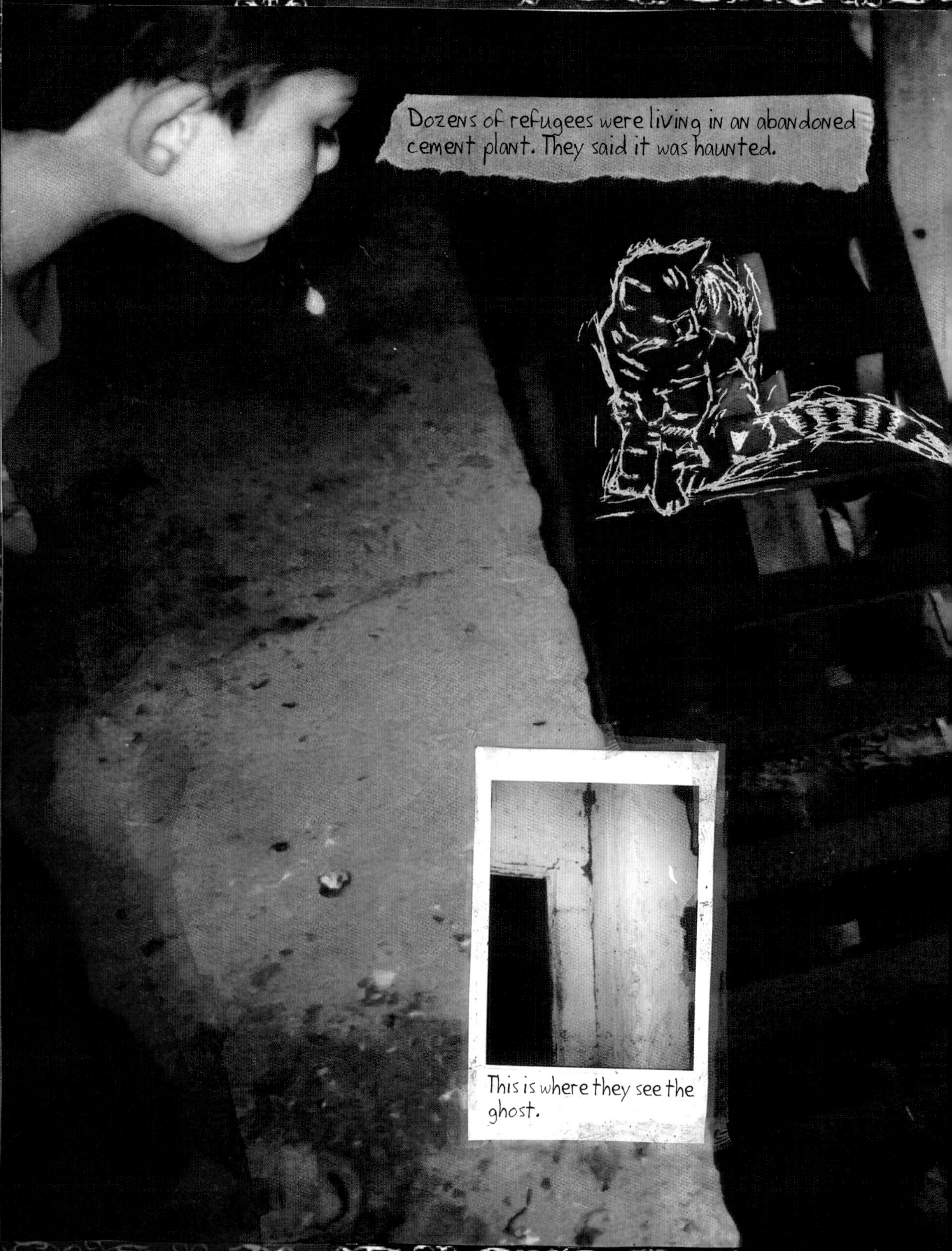
Dozens of refugees were living in an abandoned cement plant. They said it was haunted.
This is where they see the ghost.

The Ghost-Woman

Everyone here has a ghost. I am tired of it.

We play in the stairwell, away from the dead cat that has been lying there for two days. I don't know whose it was, or if it was even anybody's, but I saw it often, slinking around the dead machinery like oil on legs. The cat was skinny, like the rest of us, and had lost a lot of hair, like the rest of us, but at least it seemed to be enjoying itself. It liked all the machinery, all the different levels it could leap up on, all the nooks and hollows it could slink in and out of. The cement factory was its own little kingdom.

It's just dead. That is, it doesn't look like it has been killed by anyone, or that it died in some kind of awful spasm. It looks as if it just happened to be slinking down the stairwell and then—oh well—decided to die.

We had a cat before we came here—before our house in Grozny burned to the ground— and one day the cat disappeared. It probably got sick, said my father. And went somewhere to hide and die.

Why wouldn't it come home? I wanted to know. Why wouldn't it come to me if it was sick?

Cats are *dignified*, said my father. They don't want to raise a fuss.

Cats are dignified. Not like us. We huddle together in factories and keep ghosts.

Maybe we should bury it somewhere, says S. It will haunt us if we don't. His raw eyes glitter in the dusty light.

It won't haunt us, I tell him. Cats are *dignified*.

I am insulting his dead grandmother, and he knows it. His mother dreams about his grandmother every night. She wakes up sobbing—we can all hear her with the echoes in this place.

She's haunting me, she tells everyone the next day. She wants me to go back to Chechnya.

And then the schoolteacher starts. Talk of ghosts always gets her going. I see a woman too! She comes into my room at night. But mine is young.

I roll my eyes at S. I head to the stairwell and he follows me, coughing.

The teacher's voice rises in its usual sob behind us: I can feel her! I can feel her right now! She won't leave me alone.

If you bounce the ball at just the right angle on the stairs, it comes directly back to you. This is the challenge of the game: bouncing the ball at just the right angle.

S. won't take his turn. He is standing there with his watery eyes gazing up toward the next level. Where the dead cat is.

Maybe, he says, the ghost-woman is the cat. The ghost of the cat. We should bury her.

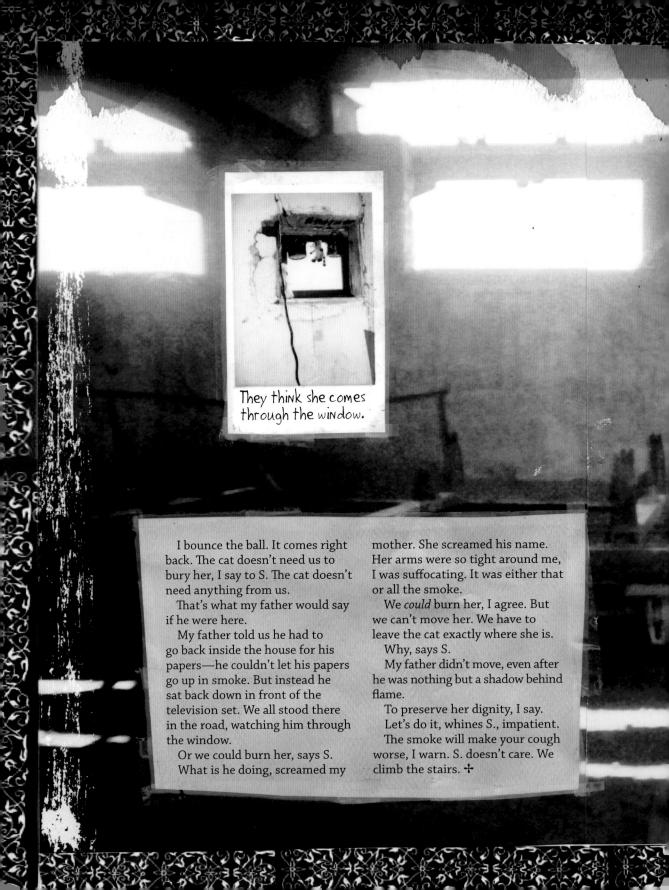

They think she comes through the window.

I bounce the ball. It comes right back. The cat doesn't need us to bury her, I say to S. The cat doesn't need anything from us.

That's what my father would say if he were here.

My father told us he had to go back inside the house for his papers—he couldn't let his papers go up in smoke. But instead he sat back down in front of the television set. We all stood there in the road, watching him through the window.

Or we could burn her, says S.

What is he doing, screamed my mother. She screamed his name. Her arms were so tight around me, I was suffocating. It was either that or all the smoke.

We *could* burn her, I agree. But we can't move her. We have to leave the cat exactly where she is.

Why, says S.

My father didn't move, even after he was nothing but a shadow behind flame.

To preserve her dignity, I say.

Let's do it, whines S., impatient.

The smoke will make your cough worse, I warn. S. doesn't care. We climb the stairs. ✝

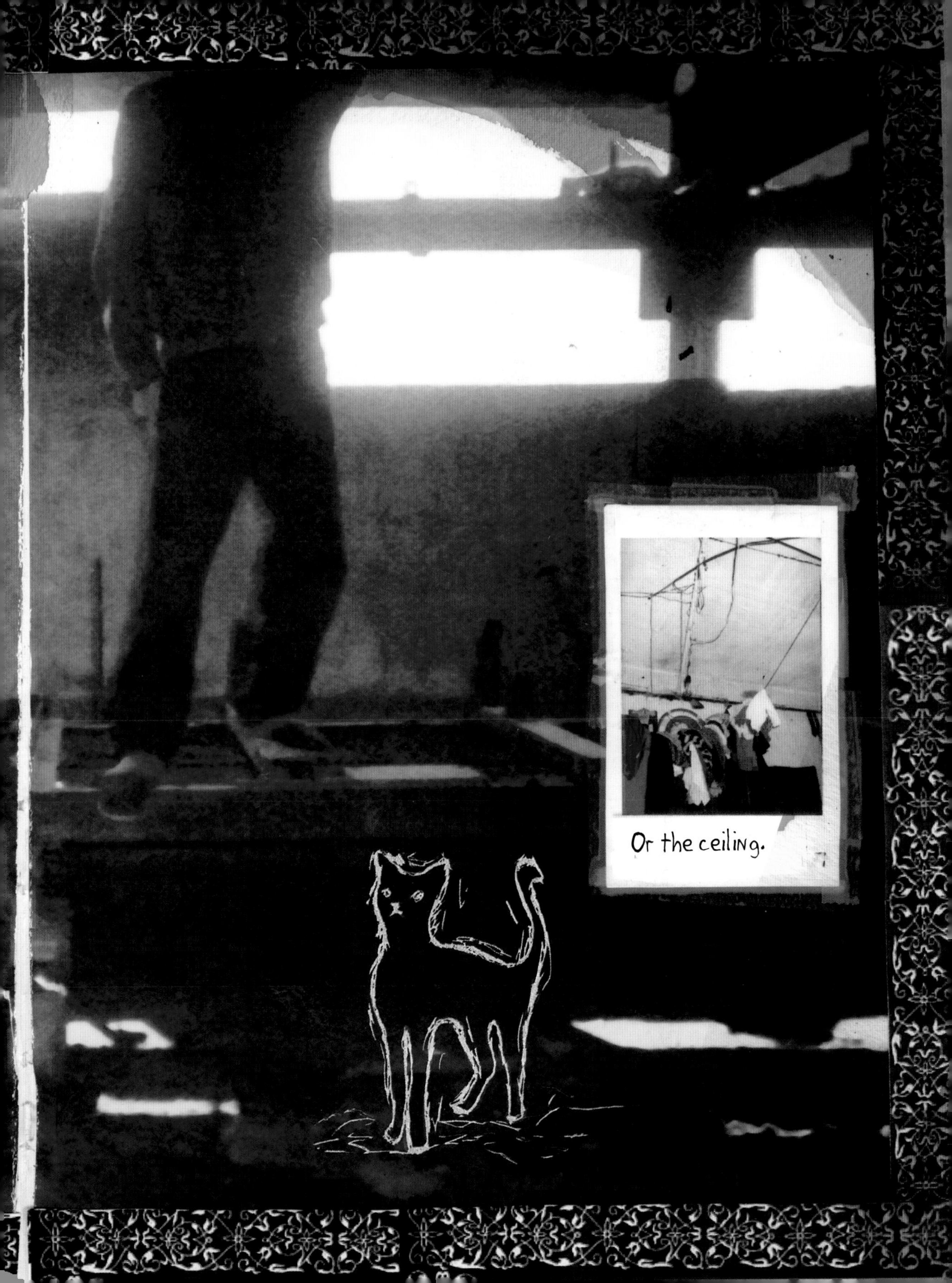
Or the ceiling.

Джабраилов Андор → abrailov

деньги money

хорошо → Good

...ошё и настрени

good ↓ mood

и — food

I assumed Ruslan would steal the camera that I lent him. He handed it back on the last day, along with every single roll of film I'd given him.

4. RUSLAN, again

What does it smell like in the room where Ruslan sits on the floor and tells his story? It smells like piss, of course. And what did he do on the night that his mother died? He slept on the floor of the train station as usual. He was eleven years old.

There is something accusatory about all the misery and death, and the mind grows weary, and every story only seems to get worse. For example: Ruslan's mother still has not been buried. She is still in the Nazran morgue. There is not even enough money for a hole in the ground.

Ask Ruslan what is the most important thing in life, and he'll answer, "Money."

There are a lot of boys like Ruslan, and they hang around the train station together, friends who compare blisters, laugh, dance, make secret paths through the scrub, run a single purple toy truck along a sheet of rust-blistered metal. They do kung fu kicks off a piece of old machinery and talk about the girl with the denim skirt and black nylons. They do handstands, get to know the street dogs. Seven or so boys, and one afternoon they went out onto the tracks to see who was a real man. They smashed a beer bottle, and then they sat in a circle and watched one another pass around the broken glass.

There is always a thread that can connect us. It's unpredictable. You're on the floor of a room that stinks of piss hearing Ruslan's story, and somehow it has all become ordinary—just another life. Then some detail catches you, plunges you down inside yourself, lights the signal fires of memory, banishes the sensation that none of this is quite real. "You must cut quickly or you will feel the pain," he says.

Ruslan plays absentmindedly with a tube of Barbie bubble-gum lip gloss. He takes off the cap and breathes in the scent.

"Can you eat it?" he asks, and seems sorry to see that you're crying. ✣

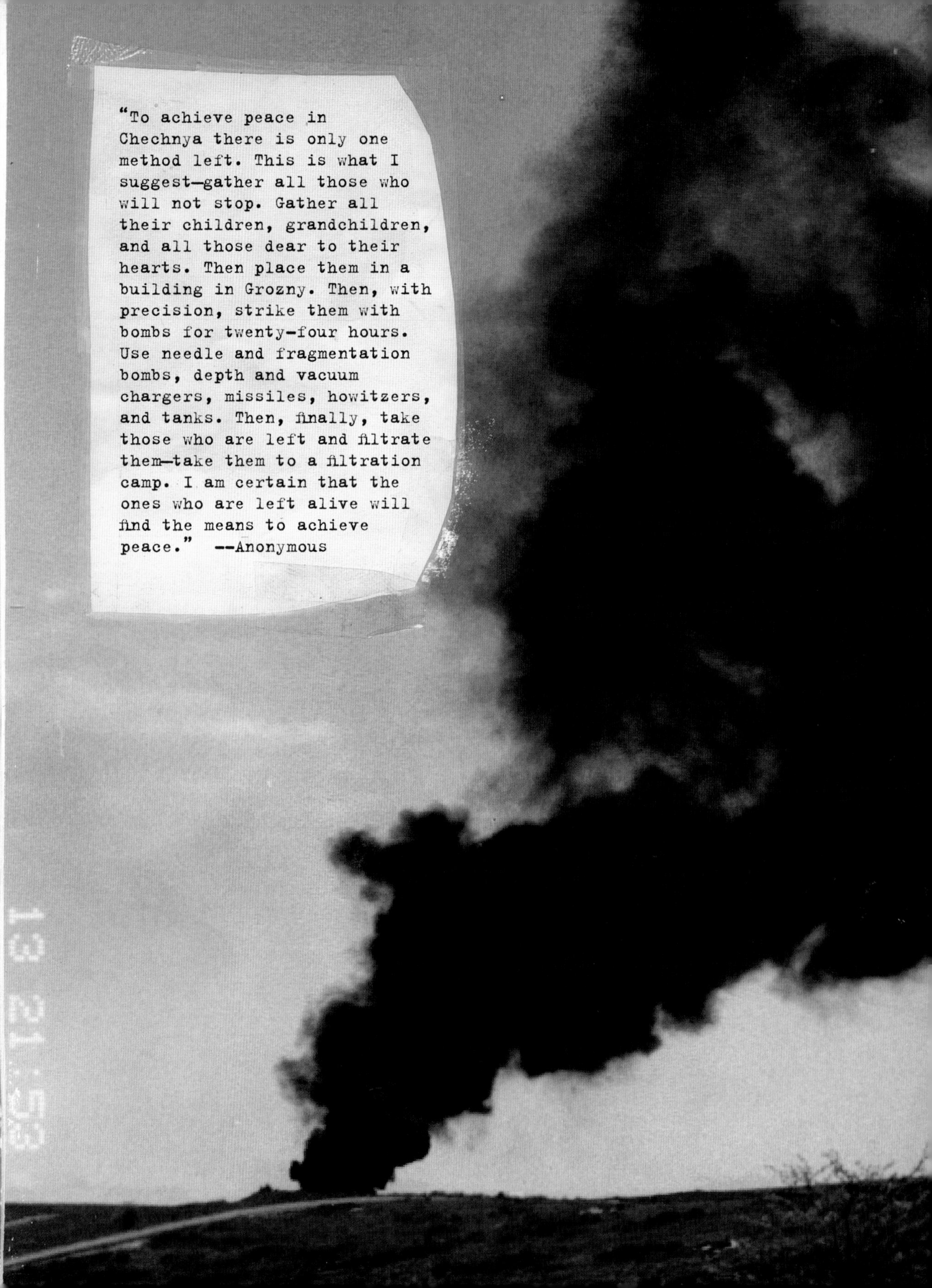
"To achieve peace in Chechnya there is only one method left. This is what I suggest—gather all those who will not stop. Gather all their children, grandchildren, and all those dear to their hearts. Then place them in a building in Grozny. Then, with precision, strike them with bombs for twenty-four hours. Use needle and fragmentation bombs, depth and vacuum chargers, missiles, howitzers, and tanks. Then, finally, take those who are left and filtrate them—take them to a filtration camp. I am certain that the ones who are left alive will find the means to achieve peace." --Anonymous
13 21:53

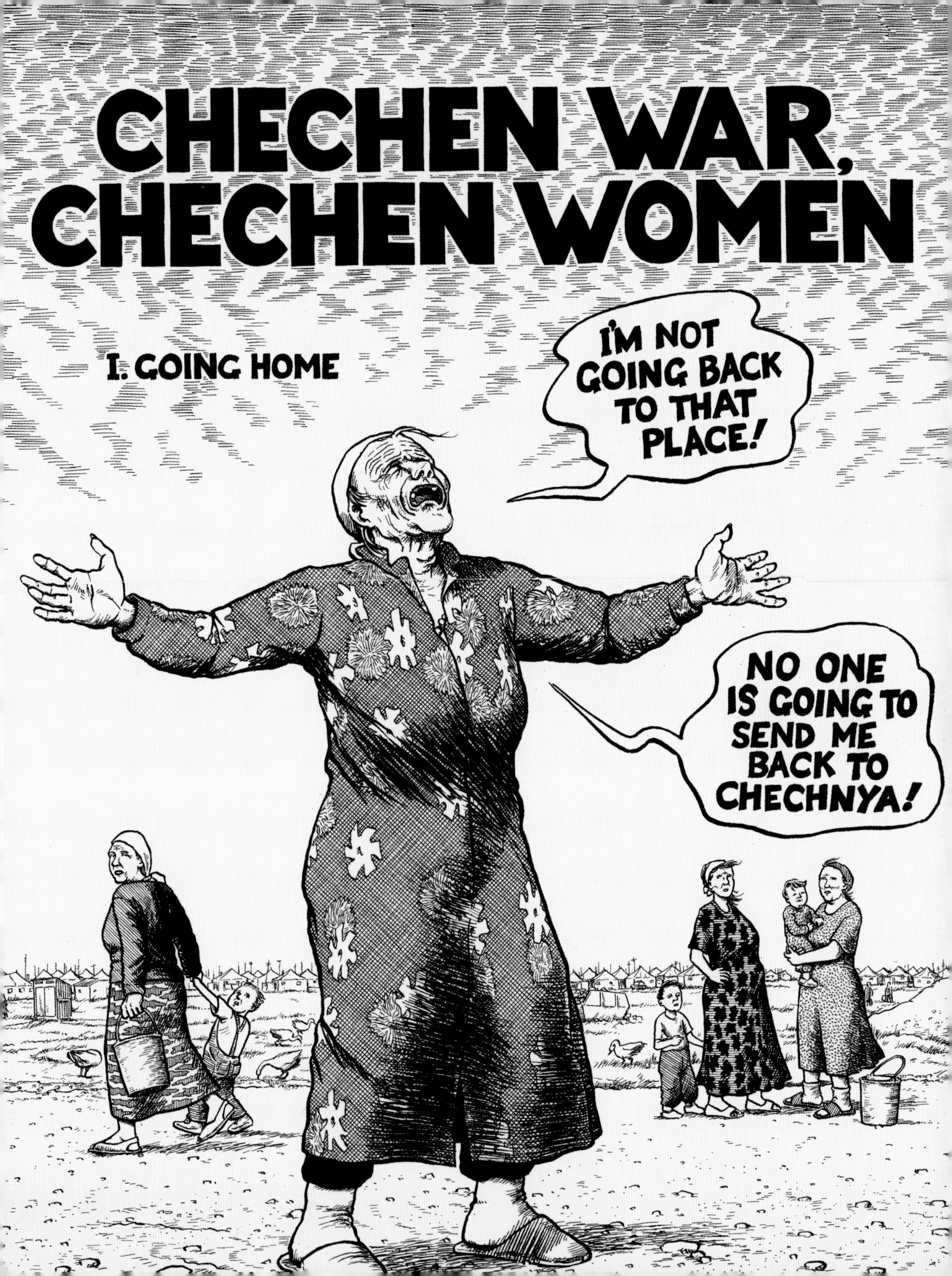
CHECHEN WAR, CHECHEN WOMEN
I. GOING HOME
I'M NOT GOING BACK TO THAT PLACE!
NO ONE IS GOING TO SEND ME BACK TO CHECHNYA!

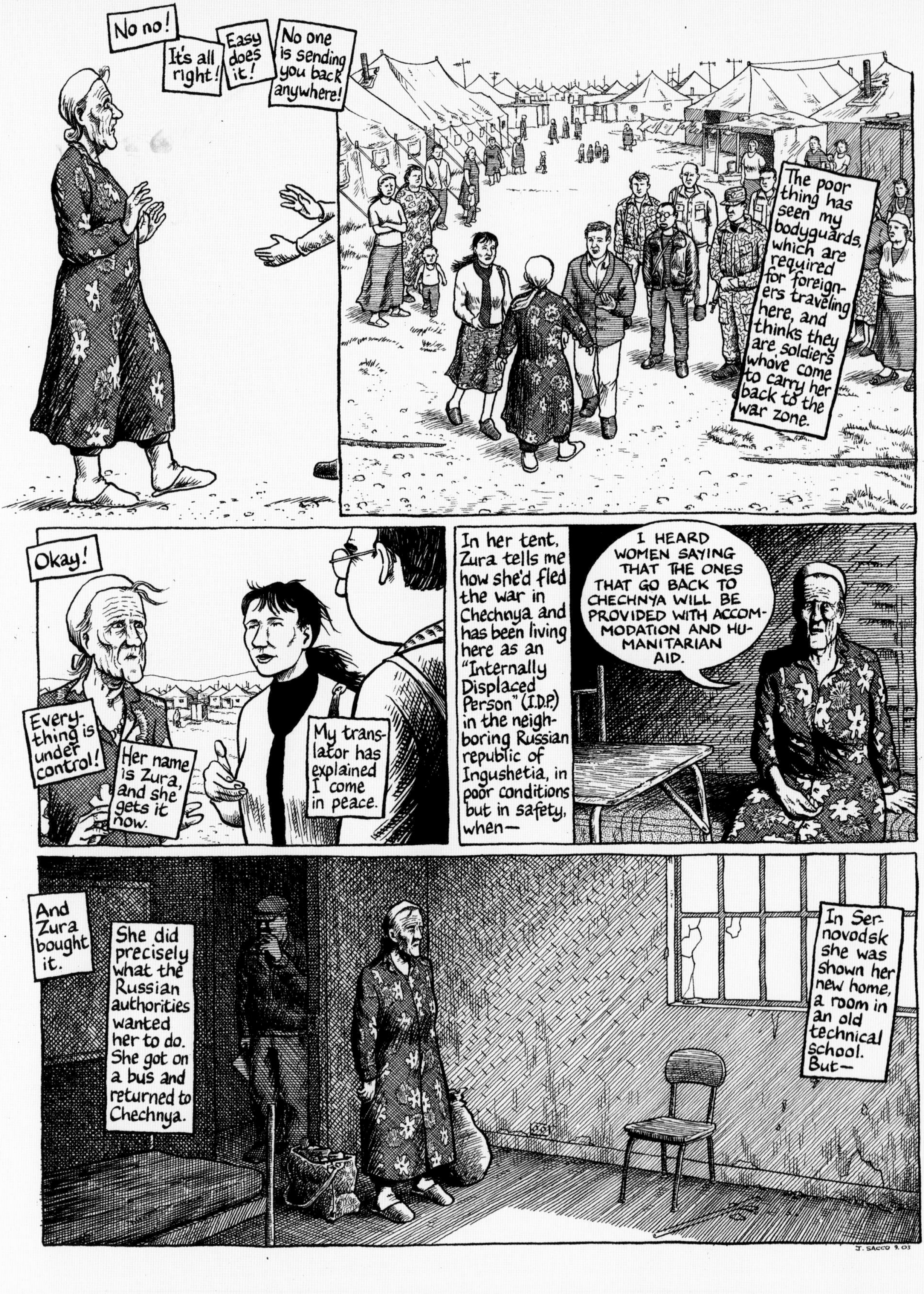
No no!
It's all right!
Easy does it!
No one is sending you back anywhere!
The poor thing has seen my bodyguards, which are required for foreigners traveling here, and thinks they are soldiers who've come to carry her back to the war zone.
Okay!
Everything is under control!
Her name is Zura, and she gets it now.
My translator has explained I come in peace.
In her tent, Zura tells me how she'd fled the war in Chechnya and has been living here as an "Internally Displaced Person" (I.D.P.) in the neighboring Russian republic of Ingushetia, in poor conditions but in safety, when—
I HEARD WOMEN SAYING THAT THE ONES THAT GO BACK TO CHECHNYA WILL BE PROVIDED WITH ACCOMMODATION AND HUMANITARIAN AID.
And Zura bought it.
She did precisely what the Russian authorities wanted her to do. She got on a bus and returned to Chechnya.
In Sernovodsk she was shown her new home, a room in an old technical school. But—
J. SACCO 9.03

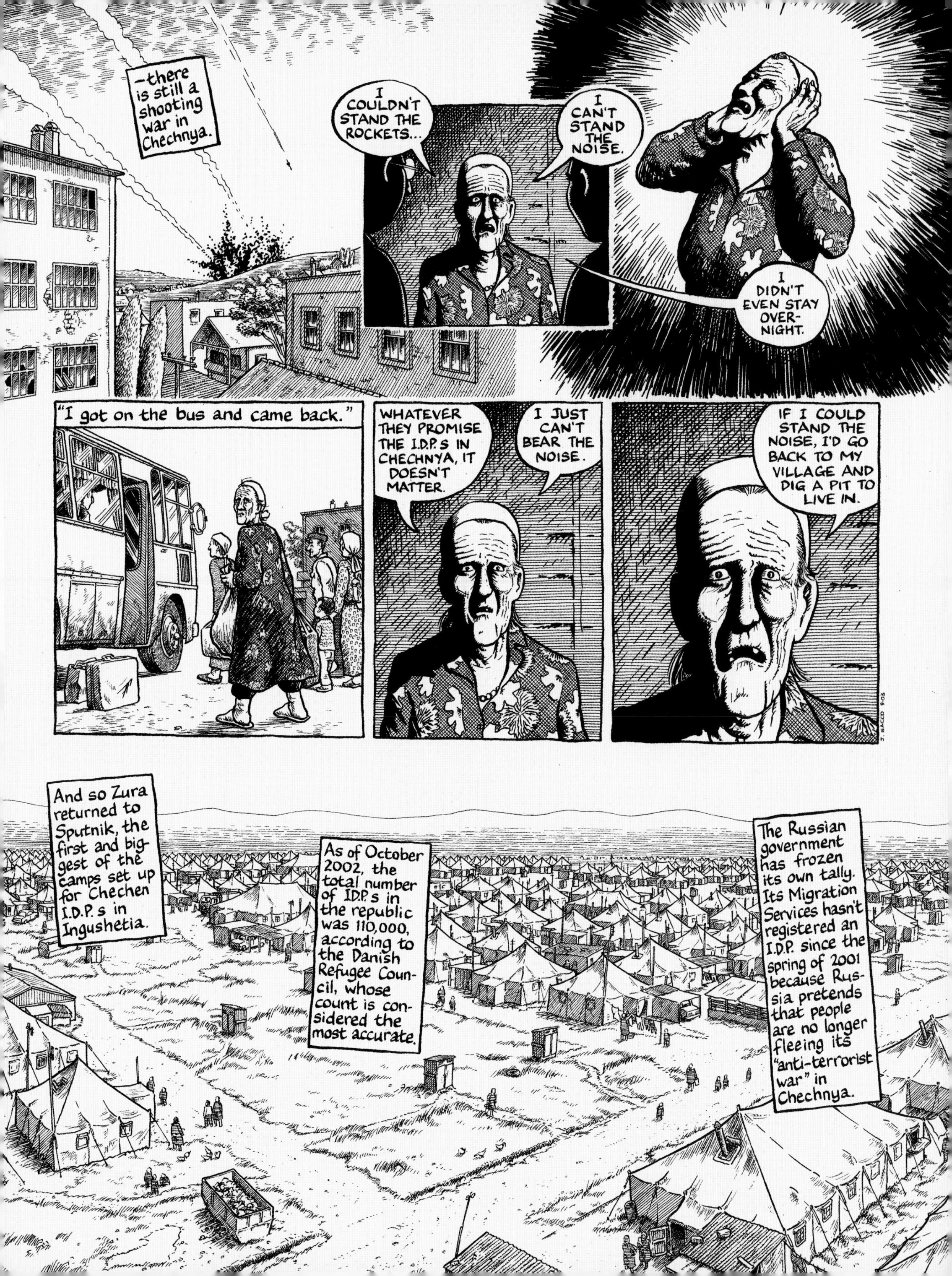
—there is still a shooting war in Chechnya.
I COULDN'T STAND THE ROCKETS...
I CAN'T STAND THE NOISE.
I DIDN'T EVEN STAY OVER-NIGHT.
"I got on the bus and came back."
WHATEVER THEY PROMISE THE I.D.P.s IN CHECHNYA, IT DOESN'T MATTER.
I JUST CAN'T BEAR THE NOISE.
IF I COULD STAND THE NOISE, I'D GO BACK TO MY VILLAGE AND DIG A PIT TO LIVE IN.
J. SACCO 9.03
And so Zura returned to Sputnik, the first and biggest of the camps set up for Chechen I.D.P.s in Ingushetia.
As of October 2002, the total number of I.D.P.s in the republic was 110,000, according to the Danish Refugee Council, whose count is considered the most accurate.
The Russian government has frozen its own tally. Its Migration Services hasn't registered an I.D.P. since the spring of 2001 because Russia pretends that people are no longer fleeing its "anti-terrorist war" in Chechnya.

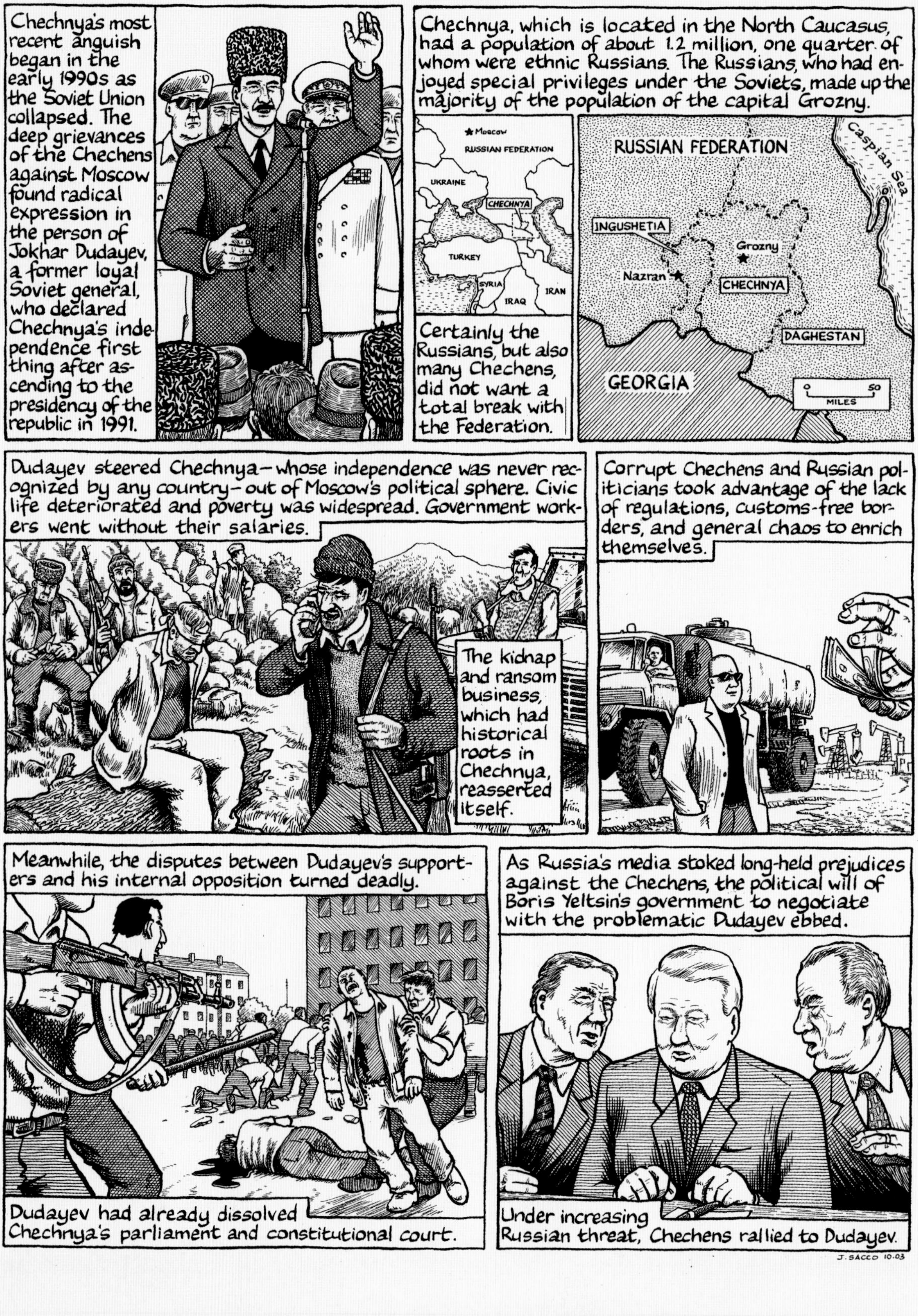

Chechnya's most recent anguish began in the early 1990s as the Soviet Union collapsed. The deep grievances of the Chechens against Moscow found radical expression in the person of Jokhar Dudayev, a former loyal Soviet general, who declared Chechnya's independence first thing after ascending to the presidency of the republic in 1991.
Chechnya, which is located in the North Caucasus, had a population of about 1.2 million, one quarter of whom were ethnic Russians. The Russians, who had enjoyed special privileges under the Soviets, made up the majority of the population of the capital Grozny.
Moscow
RUSSIAN FEDERATION
UKRAINE
CHECHNYA
TURKEY
SYRIA
IRAQ
IRAN
RUSSIAN FEDERATION
Caspian Sea
INGUSHETIA
Grozny
Nazran
CHECHNYA
DAGHESTAN
GEORGIA
0 50 MILES
Certainly the Russians, but also many Chechens, did not want a total break with the Federation.
Dudayev steered Chechnya—whose independence was never recognized by any country—out of Moscow's political sphere. Civic life deteriorated and poverty was widespread. Government workers went without their salaries.
The kidnap and ransom business, which had historical roots in Chechnya, reasserted itself.
Corrupt Chechens and Russian politicians took advantage of the lack of regulations, customs-free borders, and general chaos to enrich themselves.
Meanwhile, the disputes between Dudayev's supporters and his internal opposition turned deadly.
Dudayev had already dissolved Chechnya's parliament and constitutional court.
As Russia's media stoked long-held prejudices against the Chechens, the political will of Boris Yeltsin's government to negotiate with the problematic Dudayev ebbed.
Under increasing Russian threat, Chechens rallied to Dudayev.
J. SACCO 10.03

Russia was already aiding and arming Chechen groups opposed to Dudayev's administration though Yeltsin still ruled out direct federal military intervention to pull the rebellious republic back into the fold.

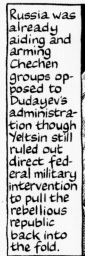

WERE WE TO APPLY PRESSURE OF FORCE AGAINST CHECHNYA, THE WHOLE CAUCASUS WOULD RISE UP AND THERE WOULD BE SUCH BLOOD AND TURMOIL THAT NO ONE WOULD FORGIVE US.

IT IS ABSOLUTELY IMPOSSIBLE.

However, newly positioned hardliners in Yeltsin's circle as well as right-wing nationalist rivals pushed the physically diminished Russian president to take harsher measures, which culminated in a military attack in December 1994.

Using overwhelming force, including massive artillery barrages, the Russians devastated Chechen population centers.

J. SACCO 10-03

Shattered Grozny fell to badly bloodied Russian troops after a nearly three-month, block-by-block battle with Chechen fighters. Among the civilian dead—estimated as high as 27,000—were many of the city's ethnic Russians.

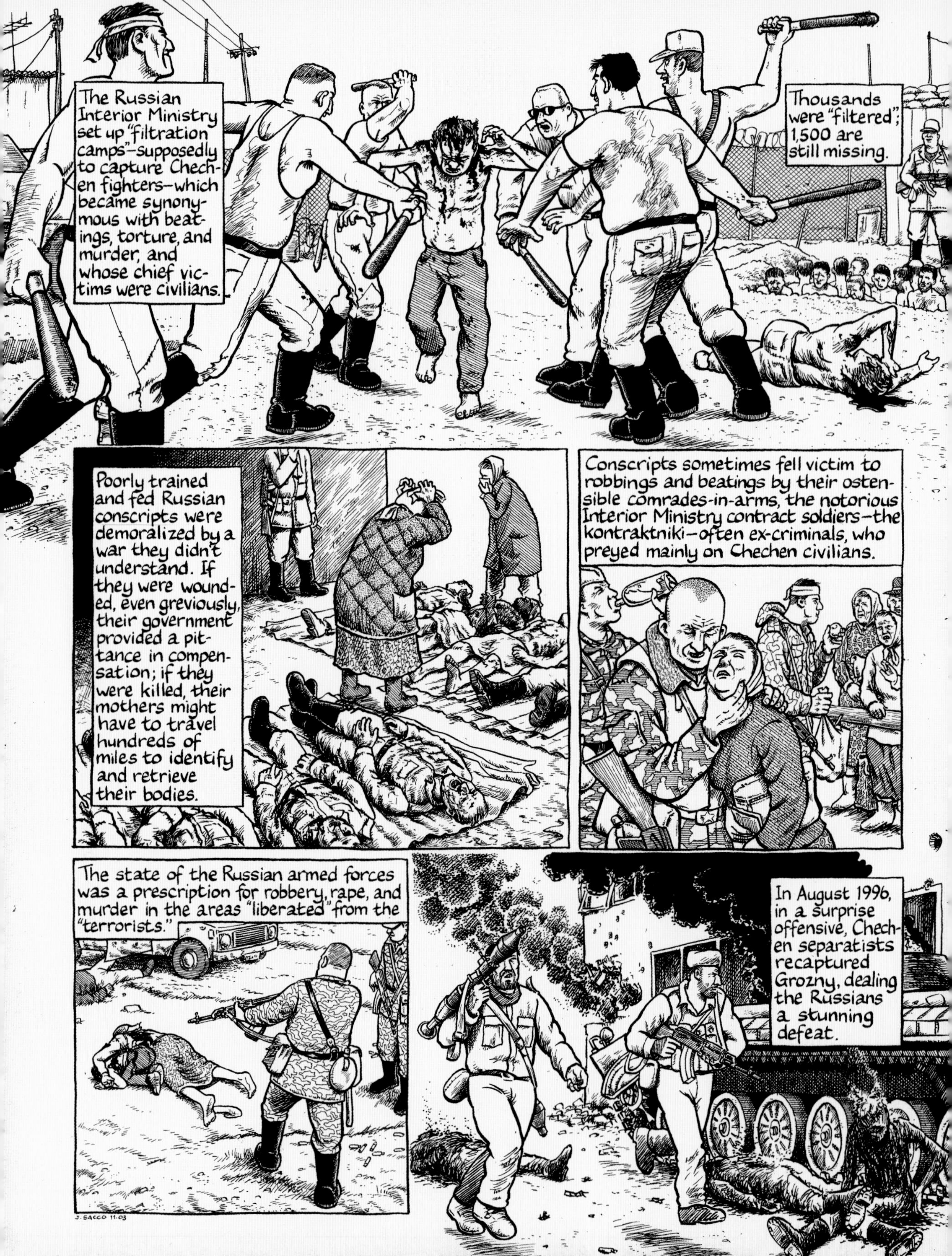
The Russian Interior Ministry set up "filtration camps"–supposedly to capture Chechen fighters–which became synonymous with beatings, torture, and murder, and whose chief victims were civilians.
Thousands were "filtered"; 1,500 are still missing.
Poorly trained and fed Russian conscripts were demoralized by a war they didn't understand. If they were wounded, even greviously, their government provided a pittance in compensation; if they were killed, their mothers might have to travel hundreds of miles to identify and retrieve their bodies.
Conscripts sometimes fell victim to robbings and beatings by their ostensible comrades-in-arms, the notorious Interior Ministry contract soldiers–the kontraktniki–often ex-criminals, who preyed mainly on Chechen civilians.
The state of the Russian armed forces was a prescription for robbery, rape, and murder in the areas "liberated" from the "terrorists."
In August 1996, in a surprise offensive, Chechen separatists recaptured Grozny, dealing the Russians a stunning defeat.
J. SACCO 11.03

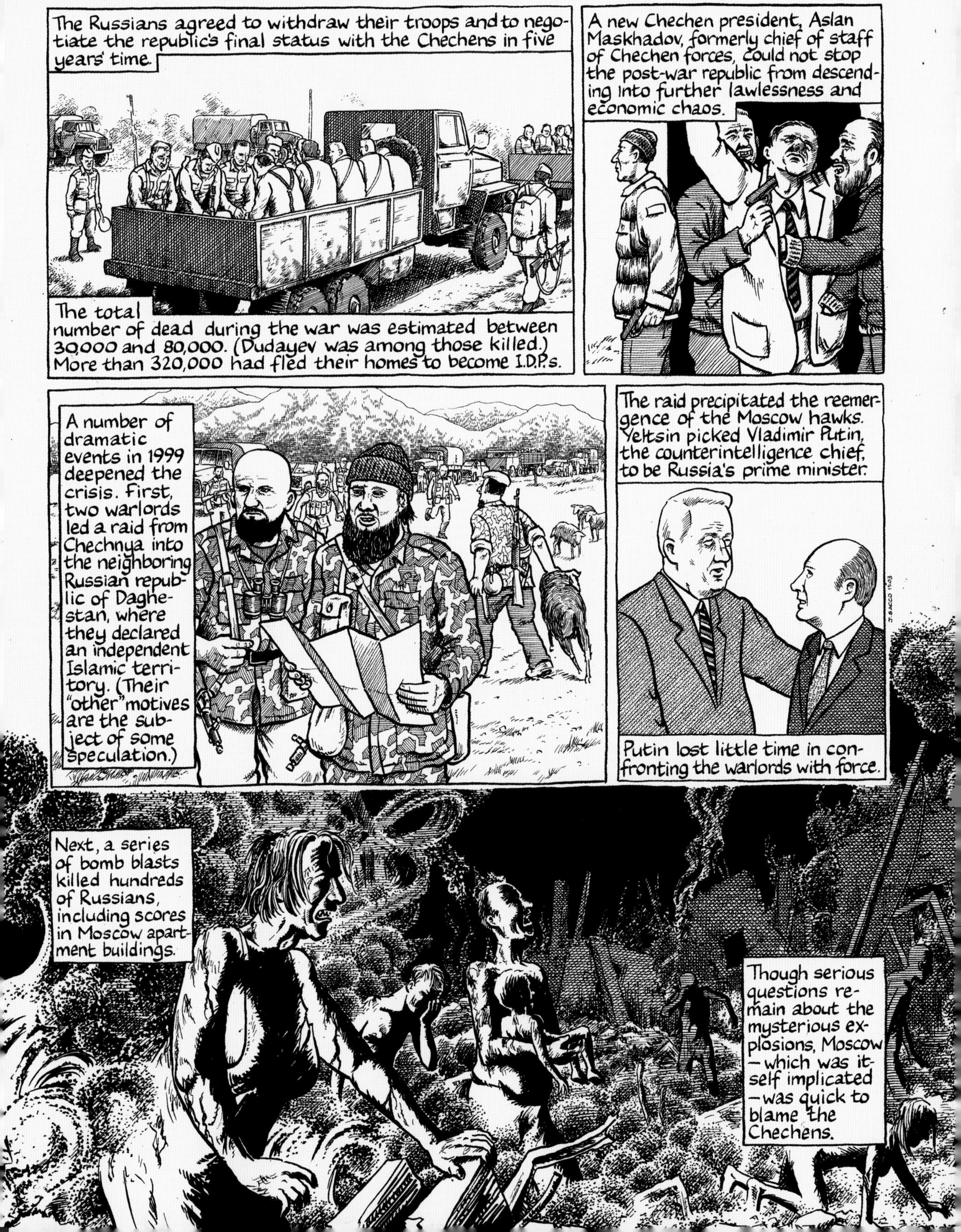
The Russians agreed to withdraw their troops and to negotiate the republic's final status with the Chechens in five years' time.
The total number of dead during the war was estimated between 30,000 and 80,000. (Dudayev was among those killed.) More than 320,000 had fled their homes to become I.D.P.s.
A new Chechen president, Aslan Maskhadov, formerly chief of staff of Chechen forces, could not stop the post-war republic from descending into further lawlessness and economic chaos.
A number of dramatic events in 1999 deepened the crisis. First, two warlords led a raid from Chechnya into the neighboring Russian republic of Daghestan, where they declared an independent Islamic territory. (Their "other" motives are the subject of some speculation.)
The raid precipitated the reemergence of the Moscow hawks. Yeltsin picked Vladimir Putin, the counterintelligence chief, to be Russia's prime minister.
Putin lost little time in confronting the warlords with force.
Next, a series of bomb blasts killed hundreds of Russians, including scores in Moscow apartment buildings.
Though serious questions remain about the mysterious explosions, Moscow —which was itself implicated —was quick to blame the Chechens.

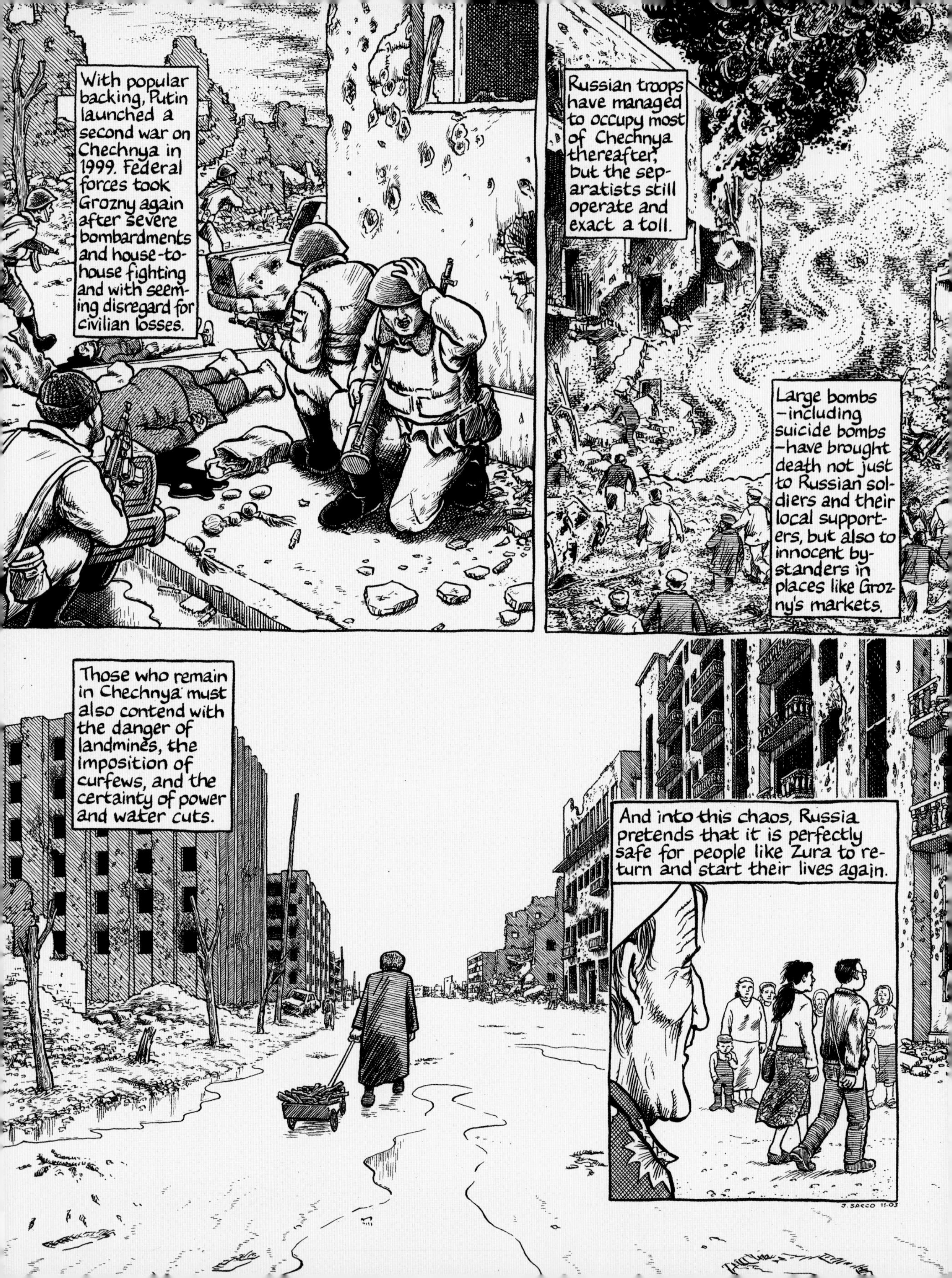
With popular backing, Putin launched a second war on Chechnya in 1999. Federal forces took Grozny again after severe bombardments and house-to-house fighting and with seeming disregard for civilian losses.
Russian troops have managed to occupy most of Chechnya thereafter, but the separatists still operate and exact a toll.
Large bombs —including suicide bombs —have brought death not just to Russian soldiers and their local supporters, but also to innocent bystanders in places like Grozny's markets.
Those who remain in Chechnya must also contend with the danger of landmines, the imposition of curfews, and the certainty of power and water cuts.
And into this chaos, Russia pretends that it is perfectly safe for people like Zura to return and start their lives again.
J. SACCO 11.03

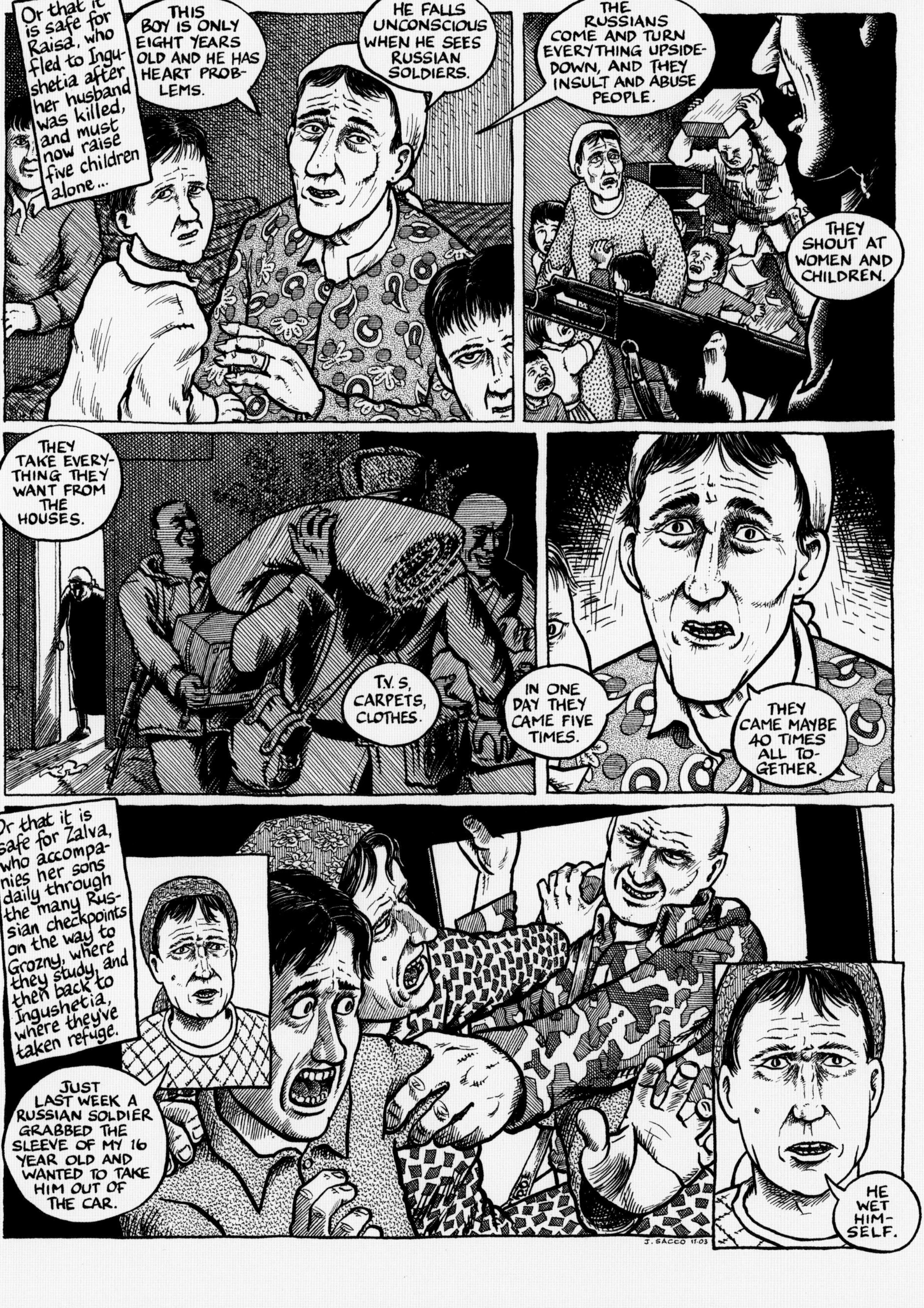
Or that it is safe for Raisa, who fled to Ingushetia after her husband was killed, and must now raise five children alone...
THIS BOY IS ONLY EIGHT YEARS OLD AND HE HAS HEART PROBLEMS.
HE FALLS UNCONSCIOUS WHEN HE SEES RUSSIAN SOLDIERS.
THE RUSSIANS COME AND TURN EVERYTHING UPSIDE-DOWN, AND THEY INSULT AND ABUSE PEOPLE.
THEY SHOUT AT WOMEN AND CHILDREN.
THEY TAKE EVERYTHING THEY WANT FROM THE HOUSES.
T.V. S, CARPETS, CLOTHES.
IN ONE DAY THEY CAME FIVE TIMES.
THEY CAME MAYBE 40 TIMES ALL TOGETHER.
Or that it is safe for Zalva, who accompanies her sons daily through the many Russian checkpoints on the way to Grozny, where they study, and then back to Ingushetia, where they've taken refuge.
JUST LAST WEEK A RUSSIAN SOLDIER GRABBED THE SLEEVE OF MY 16 YEAR OLD AND WANTED TO TAKE HIM OUT OF THE CAR.
HE WET HIMSELF.
J. SACCO 11.03

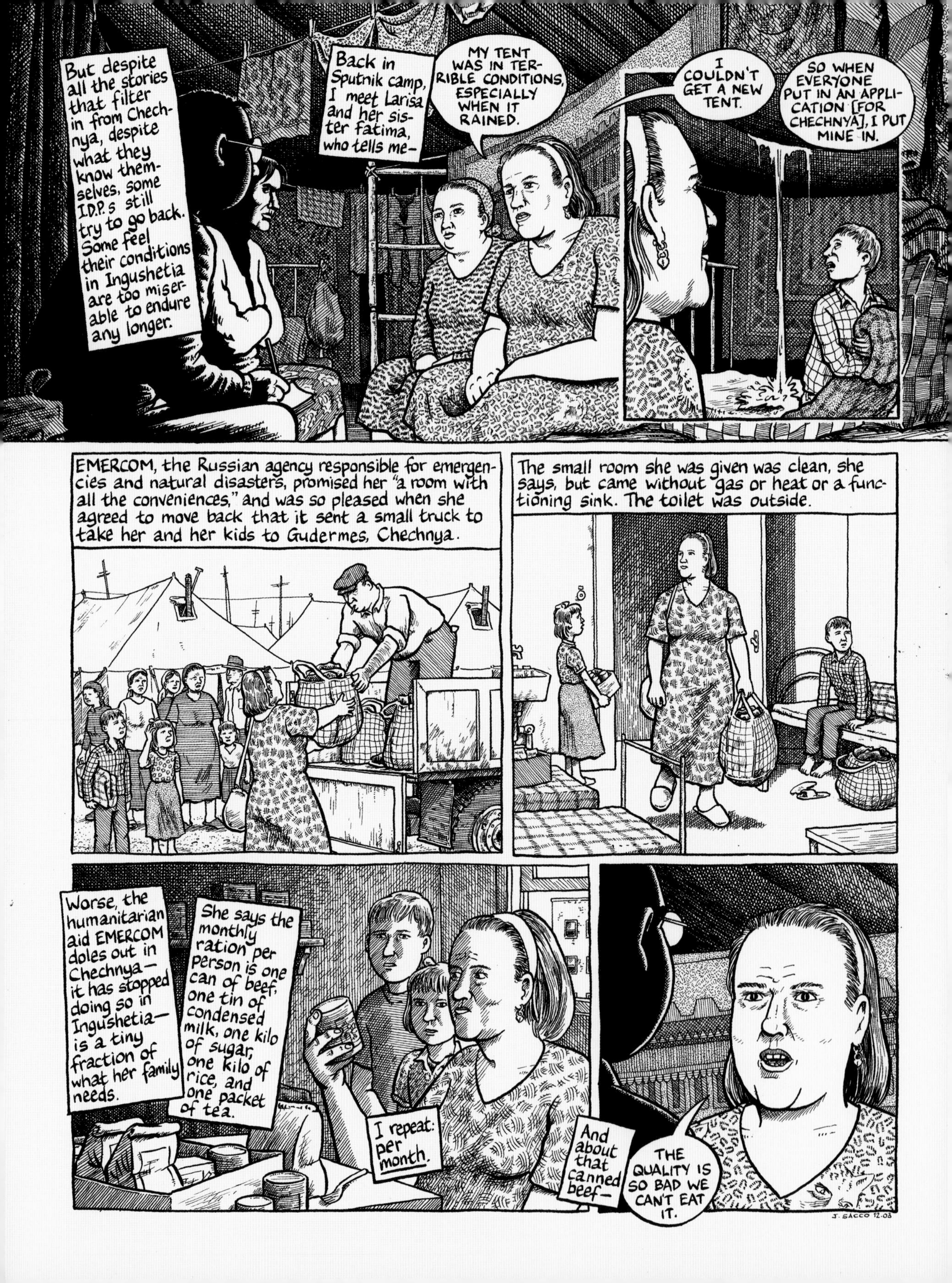
But despite all the stories that filter in from Chechnya, despite what they know themselves, some I.D.P.s still try to go back. Some feel their conditions in Ingushetia are too miserable to endure any longer.
Back in Sputnik camp, I meet Larisa and her sister Fatima, who tells me-
MY TENT WAS IN TERRIBLE CONDITIONS, ESPECIALLY WHEN IT RAINED.
I COULDN'T GET A NEW TENT.
SO WHEN EVERYONE PUT IN AN APPLICATION [FOR CHECHNYA], I PUT MINE IN.
EMERCOM, the Russian agency responsible for emergencies and natural disasters, promised her "a room with all the conveniences," and was so pleased when she agreed to move back that it sent a small truck to take her and her kids to Gudermes, Chechnya.
The small room she was given was clean, she says, but came without gas or heat or a functioning sink. The toilet was outside.
Worse, the humanitarian aid EMERCOM doles out in Chechnya—it has stopped doing so in Ingushetia—is a tiny fraction of what her family needs.
She says the monthly ration per person is one can of beef, one tin of condensed milk, one kilo of sugar, one kilo of rice, and one packet of tea.
I repeat: per month.
And about that canned beef-
THE QUALITY IS SO BAD WE CAN'T EAT IT.
J. SACCO 12.03

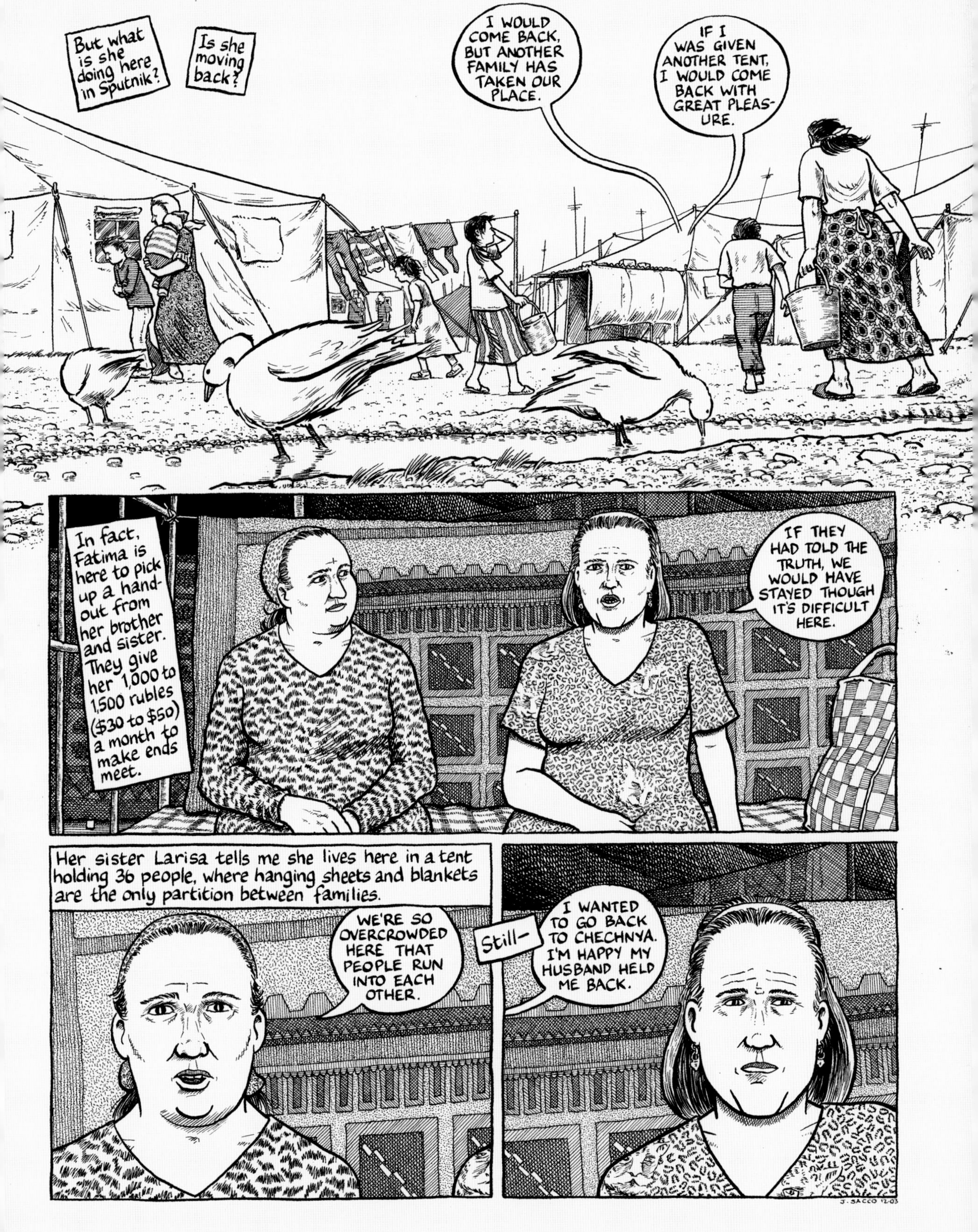
But what is she doing here in Sputnik?
Is she moving back?
I WOULD COME BACK, BUT ANOTHER FAMILY HAS TAKEN OUR PLACE.
IF I WAS GIVEN ANOTHER TENT, I WOULD COME BACK WITH GREAT PLEAS-URE.
In fact, Fatima is here to pick up a hand-out from her brother and sister. They give her 1,000 to 1,500 rubles ($30 to $50) a month to make ends meet.
IF THEY HAD TOLD THE TRUTH, WE WOULD HAVE STAYED THOUGH IT'S DIFFICULT HERE.
Her sister Larisa tells me she lives here in a tent holding 36 people, where hanging sheets and blankets are the only partition between families.
WE'RE SO OVERCROWDED HERE THAT PEOPLE RUN INTO EACH OTHER.
Still-
I WANTED TO GO BACK TO CHECHNYA. I'M HAPPY MY HUSBAND HELD ME BACK.
J. SACCO 12.03

II. EVERY 50 YEARS

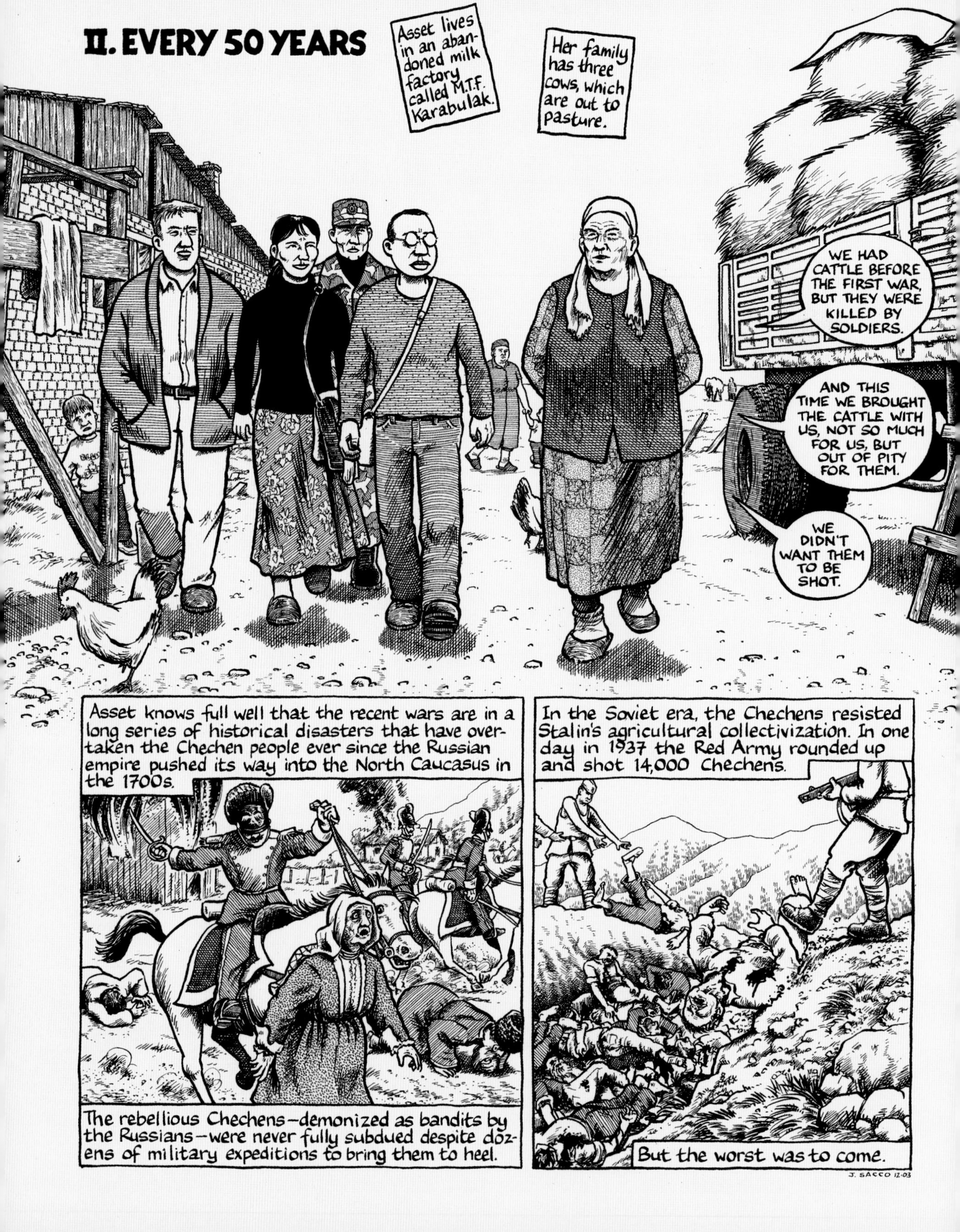
Asset lives in an abandoned milk factory called M.T.F. Karabulak.
Her family has three cows, which are out to pasture.
WE HAD CATTLE BEFORE THE FIRST WAR, BUT THEY WERE KILLED BY SOLDIERS.
AND THIS TIME WE BROUGHT THE CATTLE WITH US, NOT SO MUCH FOR US, BUT OUT OF PITY FOR THEM.
WE DIDN'T WANT THEM TO BE SHOT.
Asset knows full well that the recent wars are in a long series of historical disasters that have overtaken the Chechen people ever since the Russian empire pushed its way into the North Caucasus in the 1700s.
The rebellious Chechens—demonized as bandits by the Russians—were never fully subdued despite dozens of military expeditions to bring them to heel.
In the Soviet era, the Chechens resisted Stalin's agricultural collectivization. In one day in 1937 the Red Army rounded up and shot 14,000 Chechens.
But the worst was to come.
J. SACCO 12-03

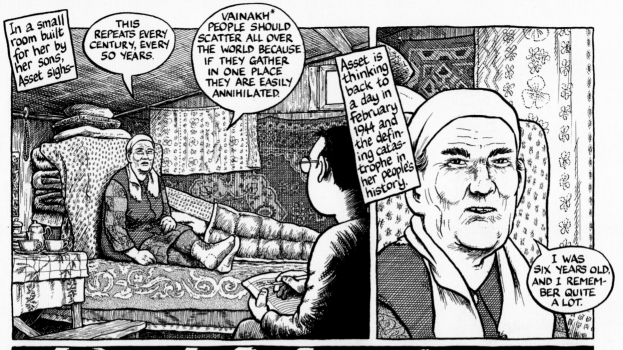

In a small room built for her by her sons, Asset sighs—

THIS REPEATS EVERY CENTURY, EVERY 50 YEARS.

VAINAKH* PEOPLE SHOULD SCATTER ALL OVER THE WORLD BECAUSE IF THEY GATHER IN ONE PLACE THEY ARE EASILY ANNIHILATED.

Asset is thinking back to a day in February 1944 and the defining catastrophe in her people's history.

I WAS SIX YEARS OLD, AND I REMEMBER QUITE A LOT.

"On the previous evening, the soldiers called all the men to a meeting.

"They took them to a storage building and locked them in.

"My mother had gone to the market to buy wool, and she couldn't reach our house because the soldiers had encircled the village and wouldn't let her pass through.

"Only in the morning did she reach our family. I remember her running and screaming and carrying that bag of wool.

J. SACCO 1·04

*VAINAKH: THE NAME GIVEN TO THE CLOSELY RELATED CHECHEN AND INGUSH PEOPLE AS A WHOLE.

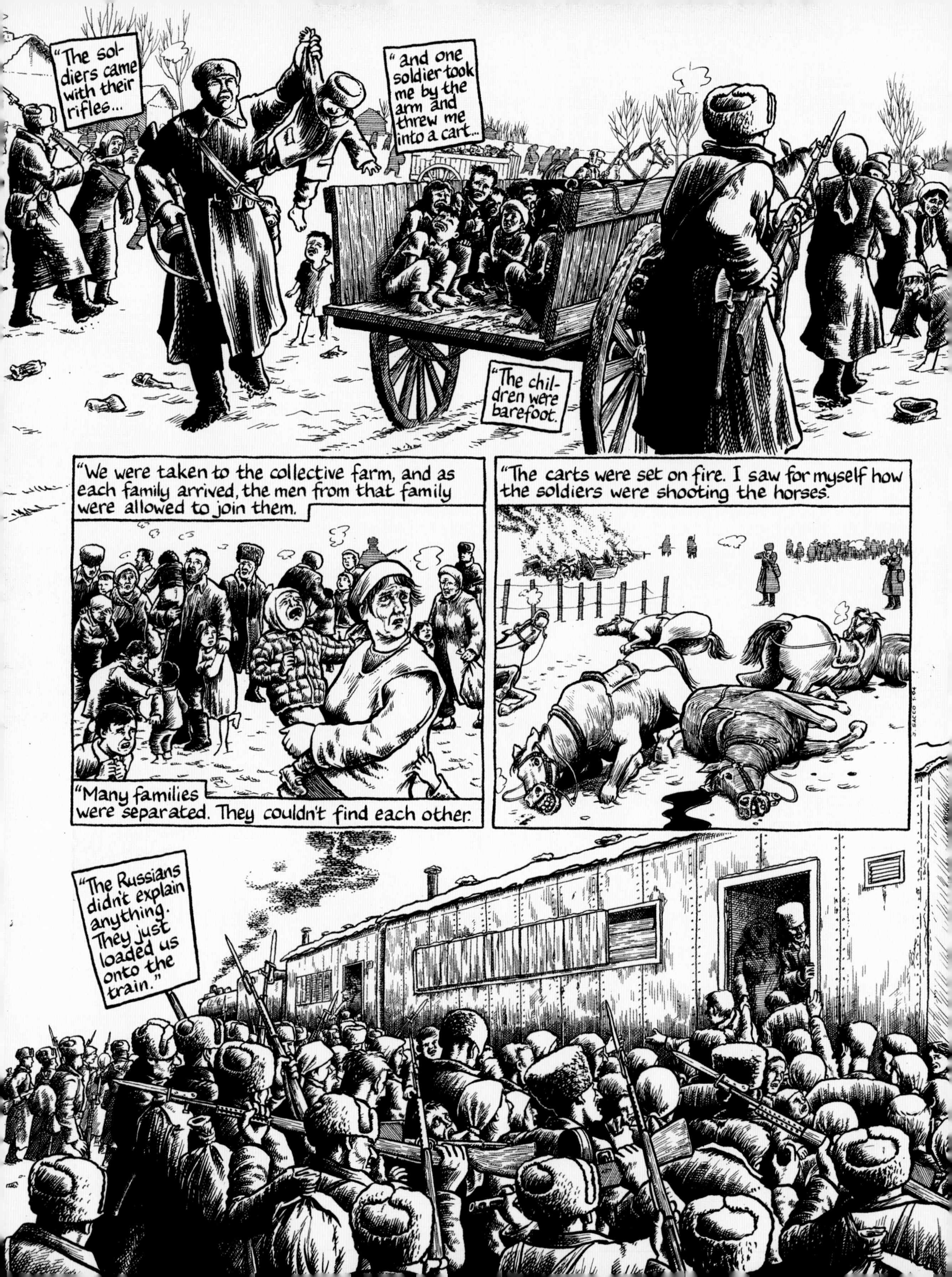
"The soldiers came with their rifles...
"and one soldier took me by the arm and threw me into a cart...
"The children were barefoot.
"We were taken to the collective farm, and as each family arrived, the men from that family were allowed to join them.
"Many families were separated. They couldn't find each other.
"The carts were set on fire. I saw for myself how the soldiers were shooting the horses.
"The Russians didn't explain anything. They just loaded us onto the train."

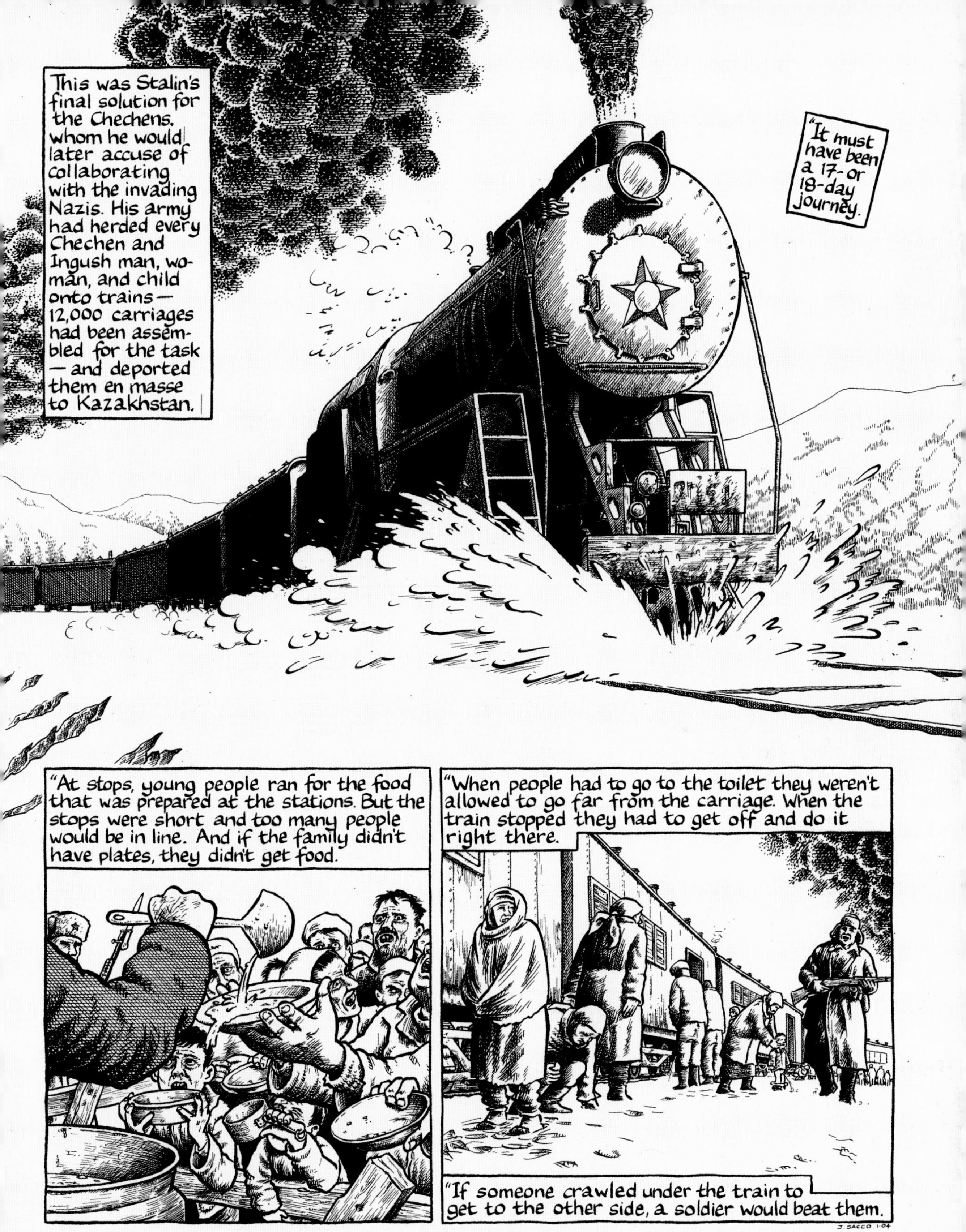
This was Stalin's final solution for the Chechens, whom he would later accuse of collaborating with the invading Nazis. His army had herded every Chechen and Ingush man, woman, and child onto trains—12,000 carriages had been assembled for the task—and deported them en masse to Kazakhstan.
"It must have been a 17- or 18-day journey.
"At stops, young people ran for the food that was prepared at the stations. But the stops were short and too many people would be in line. And if the family didn't have plates, they didn't get food.
"When people had to go to the toilet they weren't allowed to go far from the carriage. When the train stopped they had to get off and do it right there.
"If someone crawled under the train to get to the other side, a soldier would beat them.
J. SACCO 1·04

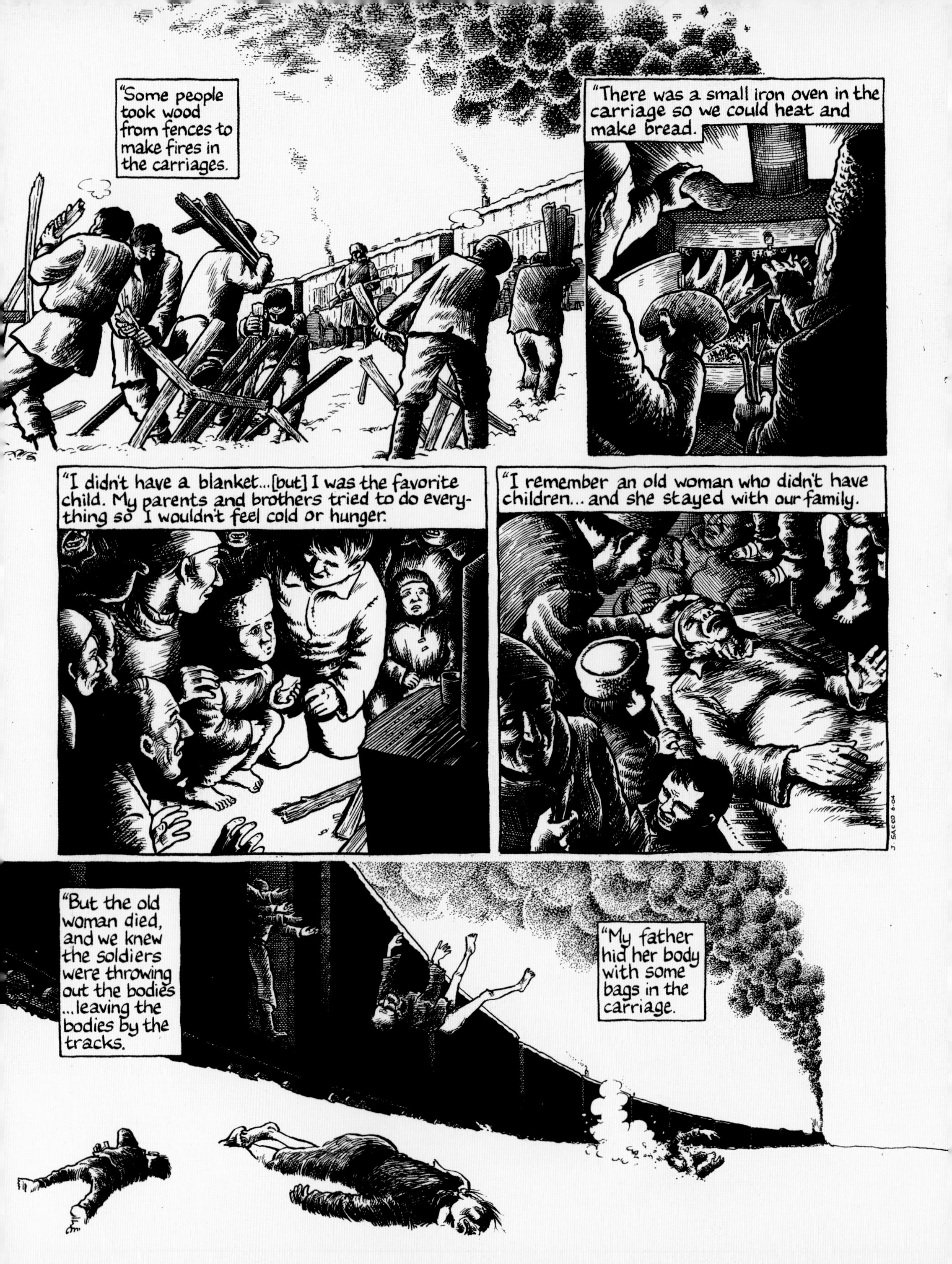
"Some people took wood from fences to make fires in the carriages.
"There was a small iron oven in the carriage so we could heat and make bread.
"I didn't have a blanket...[but] I was the favorite child. My parents and brothers tried to do everything so I wouldn't feel cold or hunger.
"I remember an old woman who didn't have children... and she stayed with our family.
J. SACCO 6.04
"But the old woman died, and we knew the soldiers were throwing out the bodies ...leaving the bodies by the tracks.
"My father hid her body with some bags in the carriage.

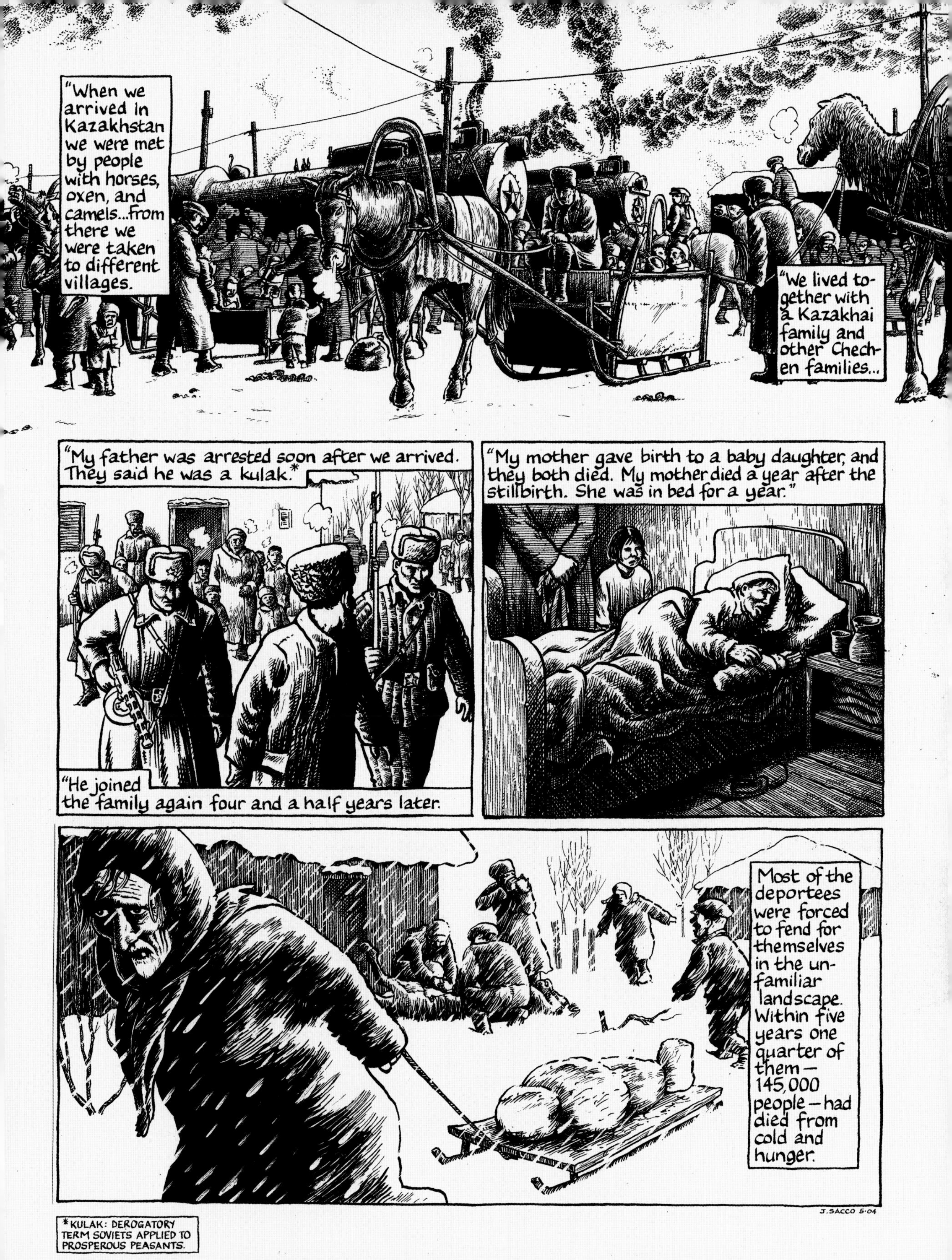
"When we arrived in Kazakhstan we were met by people with horses, oxen, and camels...from there we were taken to different villages.
"We lived together with a Kazakhai family and other Chechen families...
"My father was arrested soon after we arrived. They said he was a kulak.*
"He joined the family again four and a half years later.
"My mother gave birth to a baby daughter, and they both died. My mother died a year after the stillbirth. She was in bed for a year."
Most of the deportees were forced to fend for themselves in the unfamiliar landscape. Within five years one quarter of them—145,000 people—had died from cold and hunger.
J. SACCO 5-04

*KULAK: DEROGATORY TERM SOVIETS APPLIED TO PROSPEROUS PEASANTS.

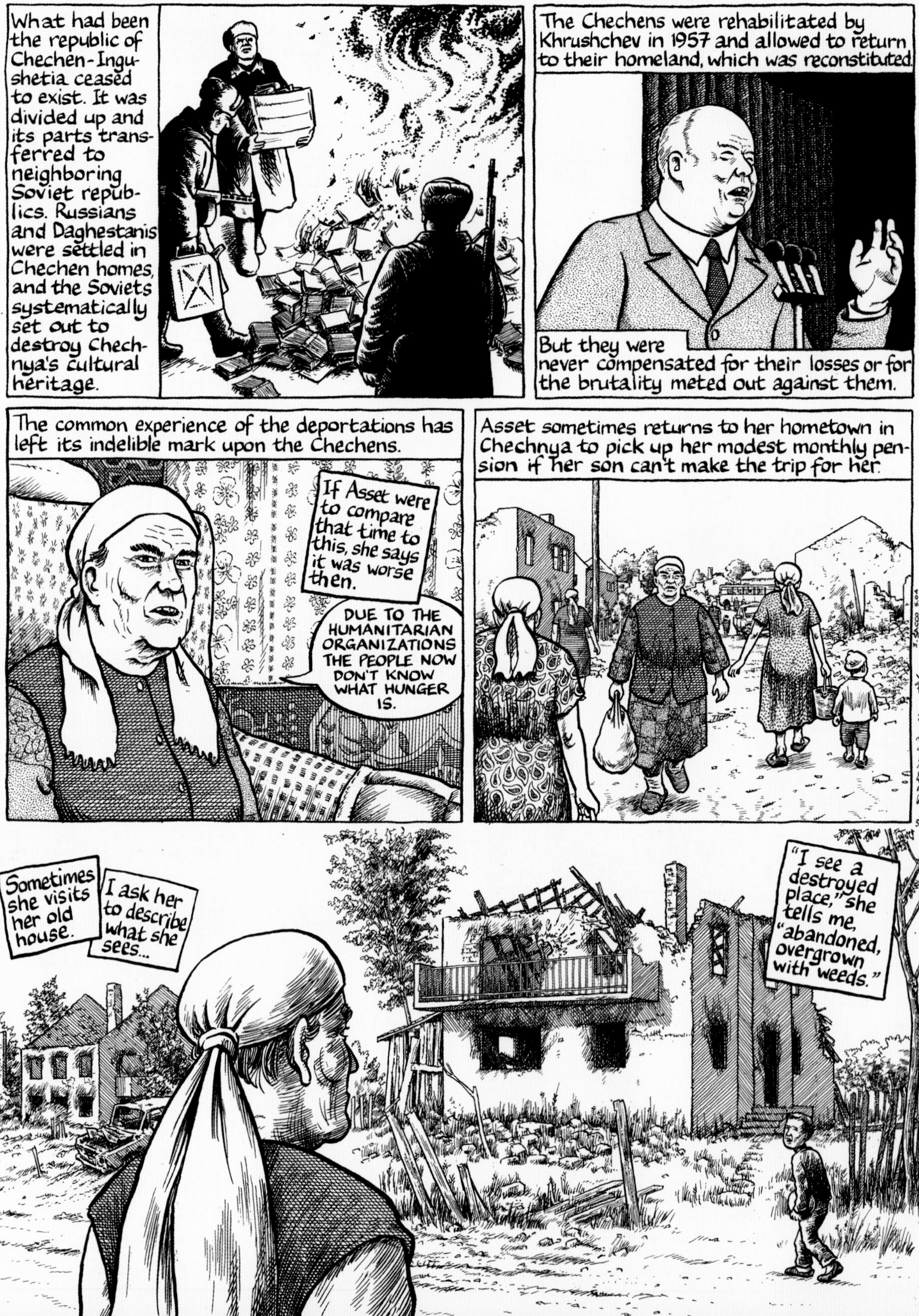
What had been the republic of Chechen-Ingushetia ceased to exist. It was divided up and its parts transferred to neighboring Soviet republics. Russians and Daghestanis were settled in Chechen homes, and the Soviets systematically set out to destroy Chechnya's cultural heritage.
The Chechens were rehabilitated by Khrushchev in 1957 and allowed to return to their homeland, which was reconstituted.
But they were never compensated for their losses or for the brutality meted out against them.
The common experience of the deportations has left its indelible mark upon the Chechens.
If Asset were to compare that time to this, she says it was worse then.
DUE TO THE HUMANITARIAN ORGANIZATIONS THE PEOPLE NOW DON'T KNOW WHAT HUNGER IS.
Asset sometimes returns to her hometown in Chechnya to pick up her modest monthly pension if her son can't make the trip for her.
Sometimes she visits her old house.
I ask her to describe what she sees...
"I see a destroyed place," she tells me, "abandoned, overgrown with weeds."

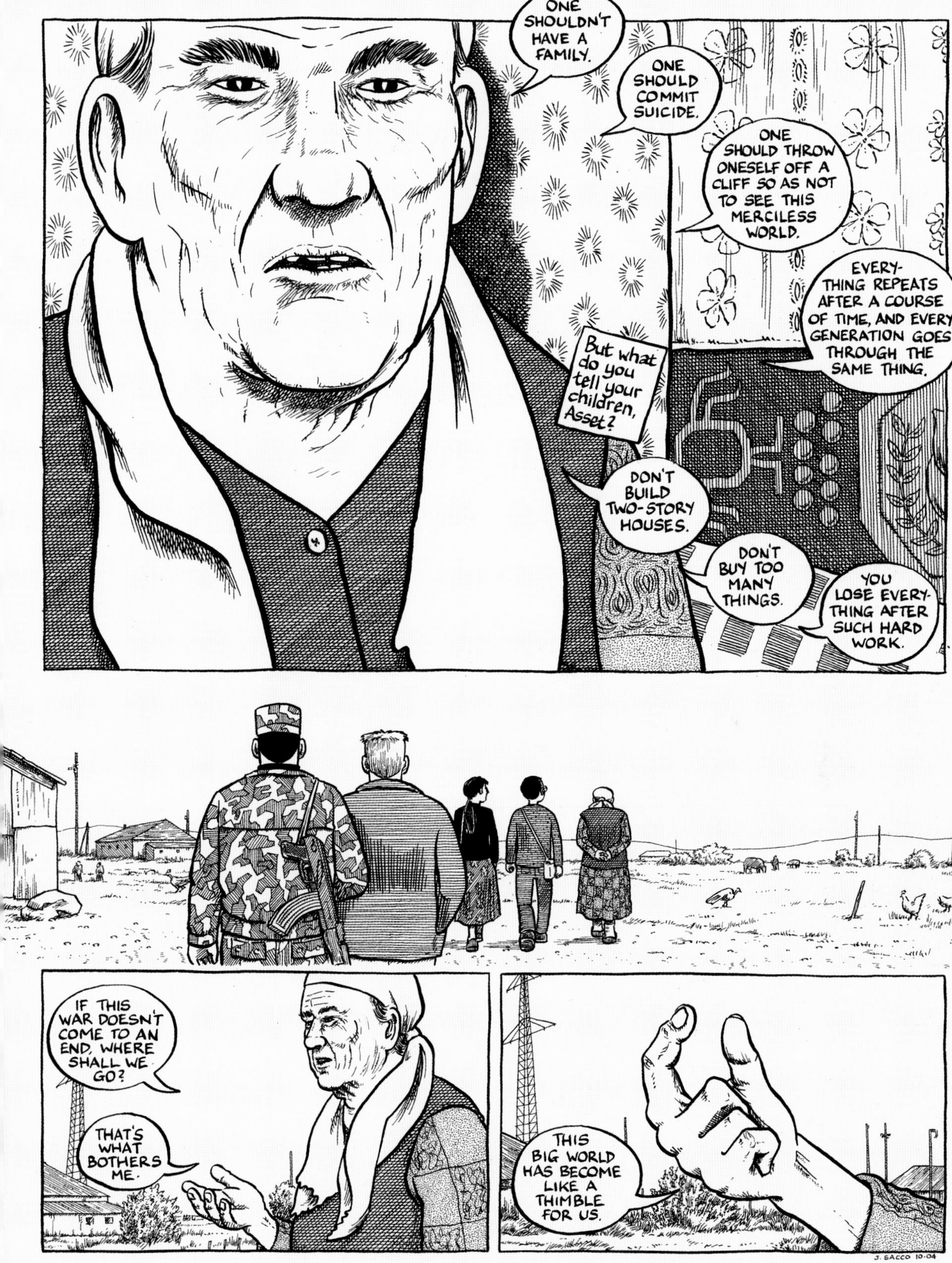
ONE SHOULDN'T HAVE A FAMILY.
ONE SHOULD COMMIT SUICIDE.
ONE SHOULD THROW ONESELF OFF A CLIFF SO AS NOT TO SEE THIS MERCILESS WORLD.
EVERY-THING REPEATS AFTER A COURSE OF TIME, AND EVERY GENERATION GOES THROUGH THE SAME THING.
But what do you tell your children, Asset?
DON'T BUILD TWO-STORY HOUSES.
DON'T BUY TOO MANY THINGS.
YOU LOSE EVERY-THING AFTER SUCH HARD WORK.
IF THIS WAR DOESN'T COME TO AN END, WHERE SHALL WE GO?
THAT'S WHAT BOTHERS ME.
THIS BIG WORLD HAS BECOME LIKE A THIMBLE FOR US.
J. SACCO 10·04

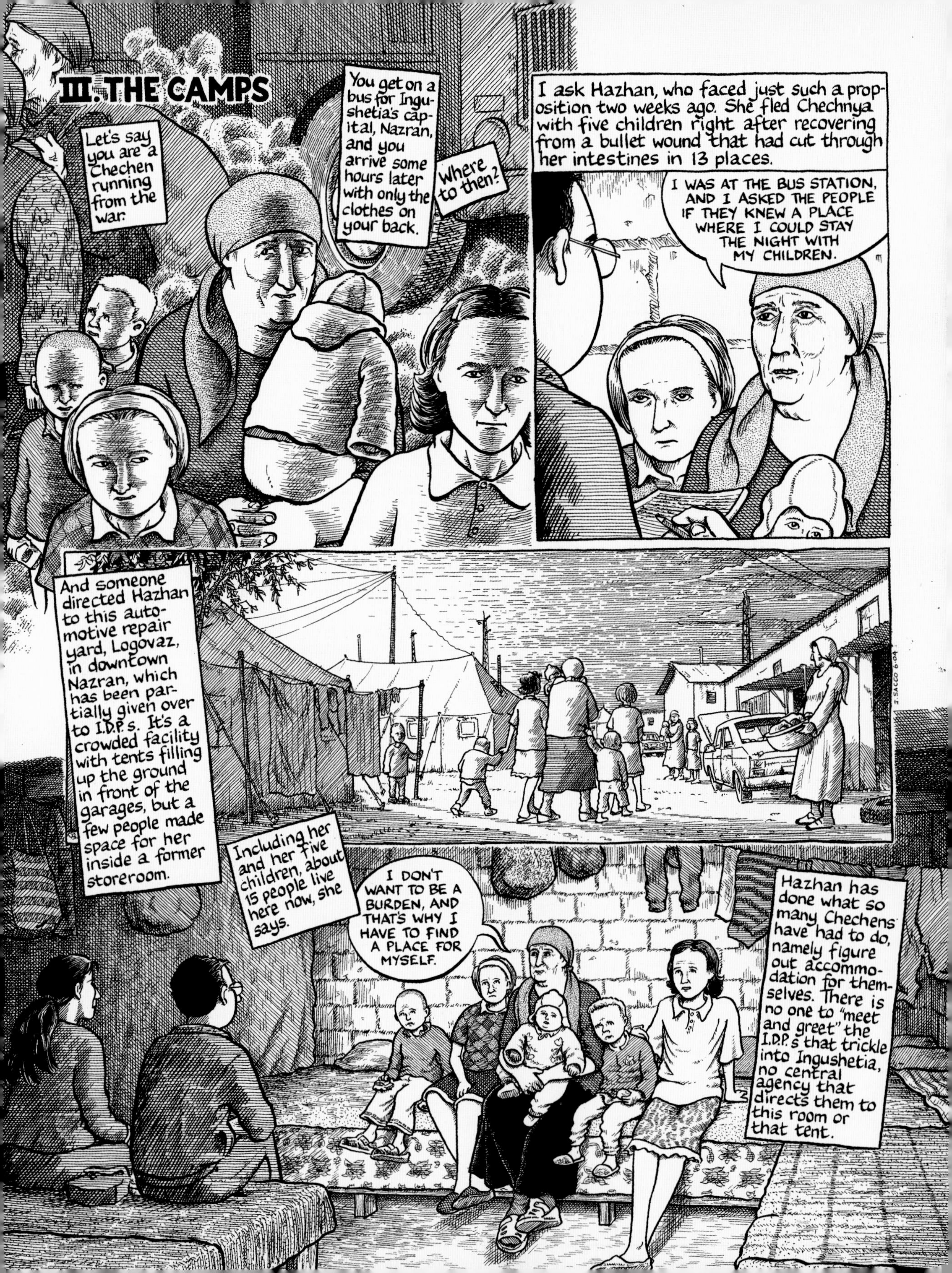
III. THE CAMPS
Let's say you are a Chechen running from the war.
You get on a bus for Ingushetia's capital, Nazran, and you arrive some hours later with only the clothes on your back.
Where to then?
I ask Hazhan, who faced just such a proposition two weeks ago. She fled Chechnya with five children right after recovering from a bullet wound that had cut through her intestines in 13 places.
I WAS AT THE BUS STATION, AND I ASKED THE PEOPLE IF THEY KNEW A PLACE WHERE I COULD STAY THE NIGHT WITH MY CHILDREN.
And someone directed Hazhan to this automotive repair yard, Logovaz, in downtown Nazran, which has been partially given over to I.D.P.s. It's a crowded facility with tents filling up the ground in front of the garages, but a few people made space for her inside a former storeroom.
J. SACCO 6-04
Including her and her five children, about 15 people live here now, she says.
I DON'T WANT TO BE A BURDEN, AND THAT'S WHY I HAVE TO FIND A PLACE FOR MYSELF.
Hazhan has done what so many Chechens have had to do, namely figure out accommodation for themselves. There is no one to "meet and greet" the I.D.P.s that trickle into Ingushetia, no central agency that directs them to this room or that tent.

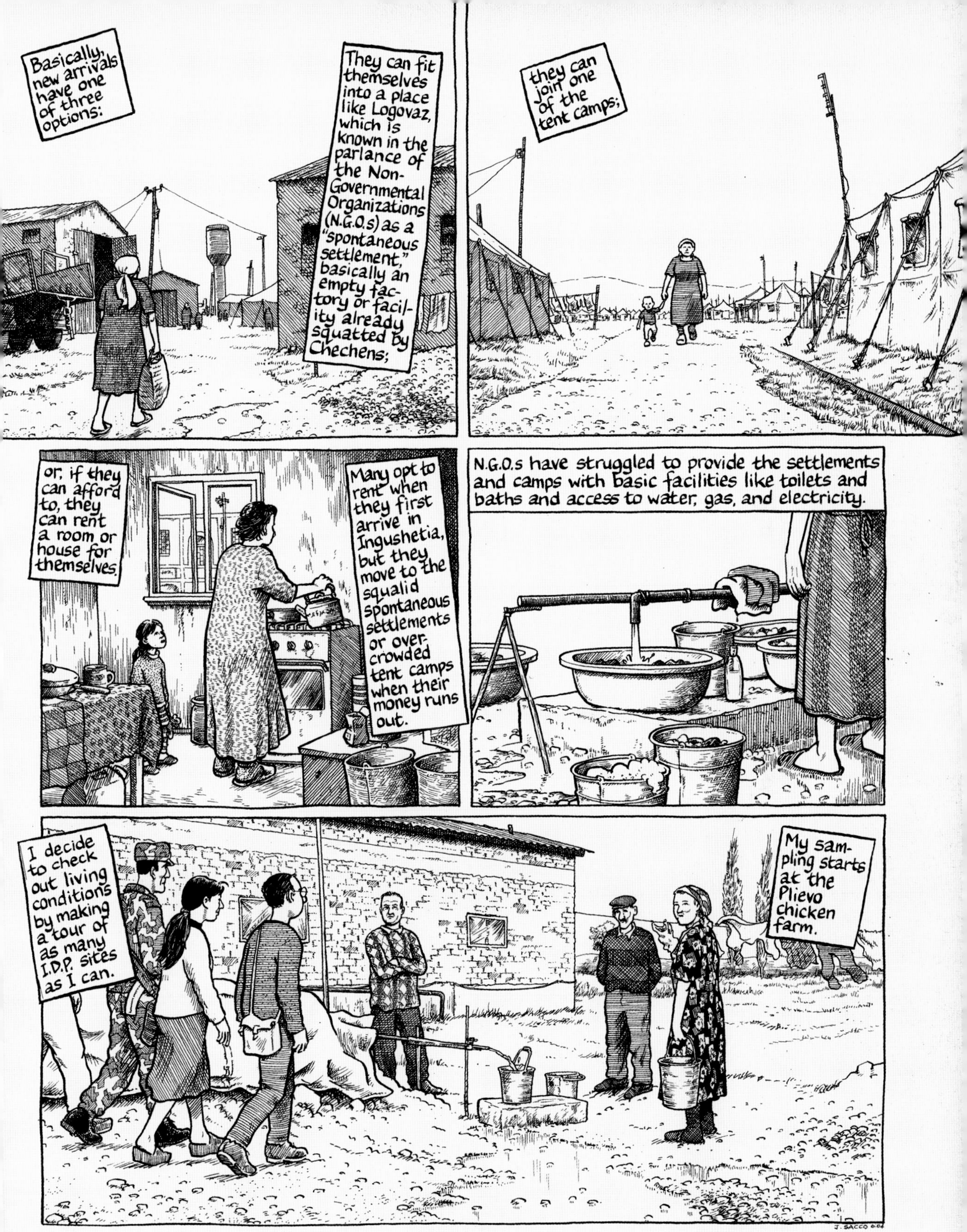

Basically, new arrivals have one of three options:
They can fit themselves into a place like Logovaz, which is known in the parlance of the Non-Governmental Organizations (N.G.O.s) as a "spontaneous settlement," basically an empty factory or facility already squatted by Chechens;
they can join one of the tent camps;
or, if they can afford to, they can rent a room or house for themselves.
Many opt to rent when they first arrive in Ingushetia, but they move to the squalid spontaneous settlements or overcrowded tent camps when their money runs out.
N.G.O.s have struggled to provide the settlements and camps with basic facilities like toilets and baths and access to water, gas, and electricity.
I decide to check out living conditions by making a tour of as many I.D.P. sites as I can.
My sampling starts at the Plievo chicken farm.
J. SACCO 6.04

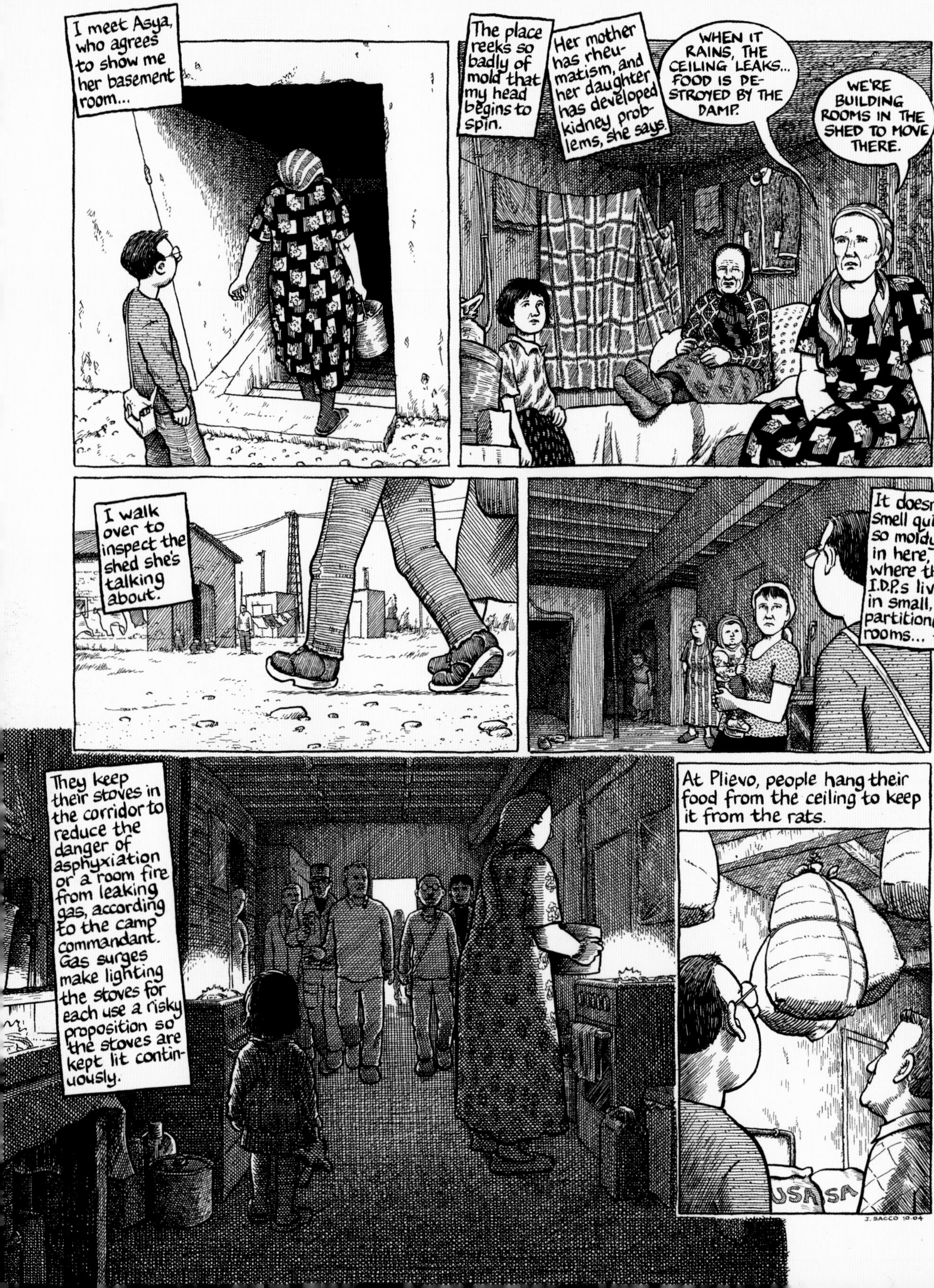
I meet Asya, who agrees to show me her basement room...
The place reeks so badly of mold that my head begins to spin.
Her mother has rheumatism, and her daughter has developed kidney problems, she says.
WHEN IT RAINS, THE CEILING LEAKS... FOOD IS DESTROYED BY THE DAMP.
WE'RE BUILDING ROOMS IN THE SHED TO MOVE THERE.
I walk over to inspect the shed she's talking about.
It doesn't smell quite so moldy in here, where the I.D.P.s live in small, partitioned rooms...
They keep their stoves in the corridor to reduce the danger of asphyxiation or a room fire from leaking gas, according to the camp commandant. Gas surges make lighting the stoves for each use a risky proposition so the stoves are kept lit continuously.
At Plievo, people hang their food from the ceiling to keep it from the rats.
USA
SA
J. SACCO 10.04

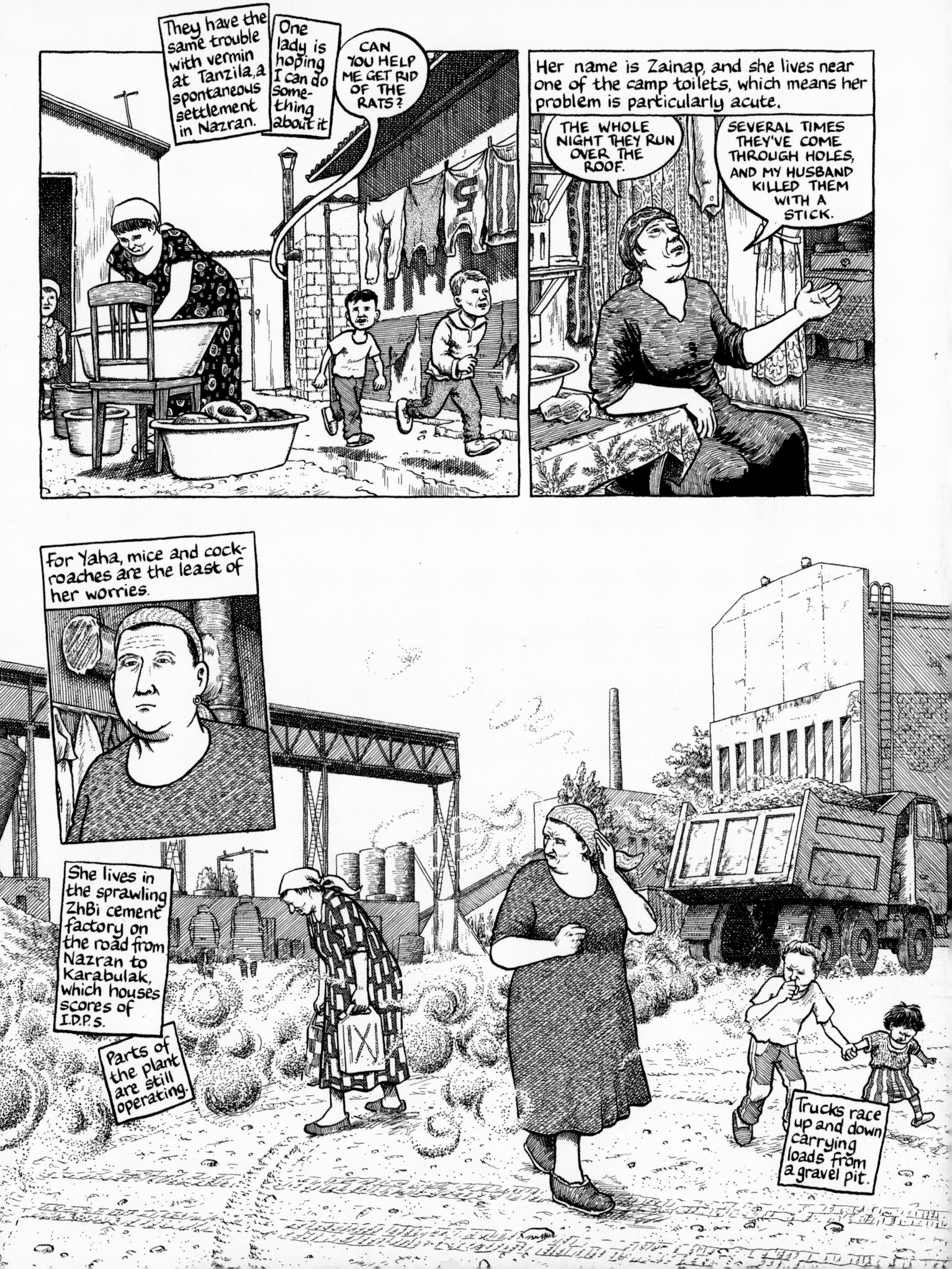
They have the same trouble with vermin at Tanzila, a spontaneous settlement in Nazran.
One lady is hoping I can do something about it
CAN YOU HELP ME GET RID OF THE RATS?
Her name is Zainap, and she lives near one of the camp toilets, which means her problem is particularly acute.
THE WHOLE NIGHT THEY RUN OVER THE ROOF.
SEVERAL TIMES THEY'VE COME THROUGH HOLES, AND MY HUSBAND KILLED THEM WITH A STICK.
For Yaha, mice and cockroaches are the least of her worries.
She lives in the sprawling ZhBi cement factory on the road from Nazran to Karabulak, which houses scores of I.D.P.s.
Parts of the plant are still operating.
Trucks race up and down carrying loads from a gravel pit.

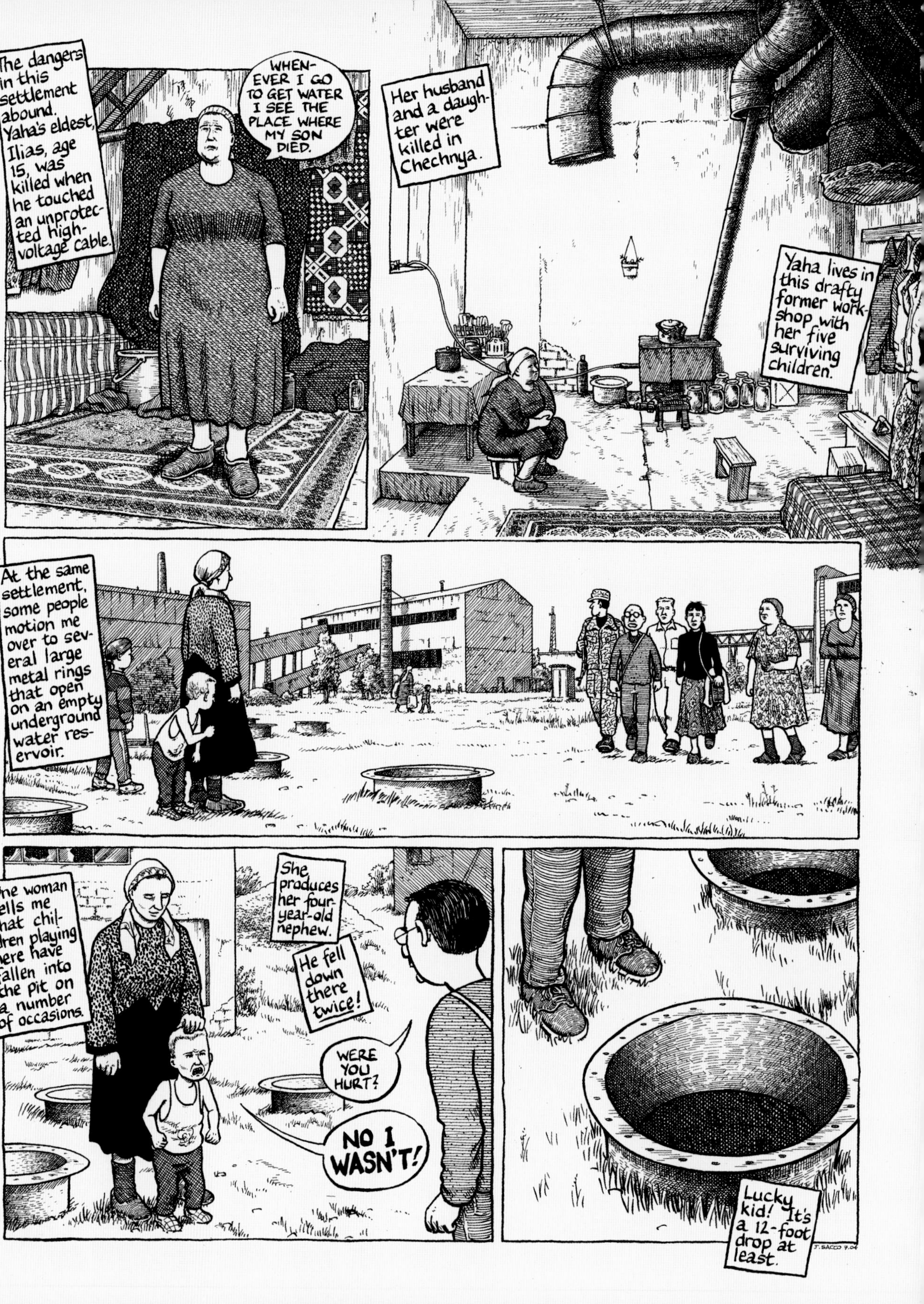

The dangers in this settlement abound. Yaha's eldest, Ilias, age 15, was killed when he touched an unprotected high-voltage cable.
WHENEVER I GO TO GET WATER I SEE THE PLACE WHERE MY SON DIED.
Her husband and a daughter were killed in Chechnya.
Yaha lives in this drafty former workshop with her five surviving children.
At the same settlement, some people motion me over to several large metal rings that open on an empty underground water reservoir.
One woman tells me that children playing here have fallen into the pit on a number of occasions.
She produces her four-year-old nephew.
He fell down there twice!
WERE YOU HURT?
NO I WASN'T!
Lucky kid! It's a 12-foot drop at least.
J. SACCO 7.04

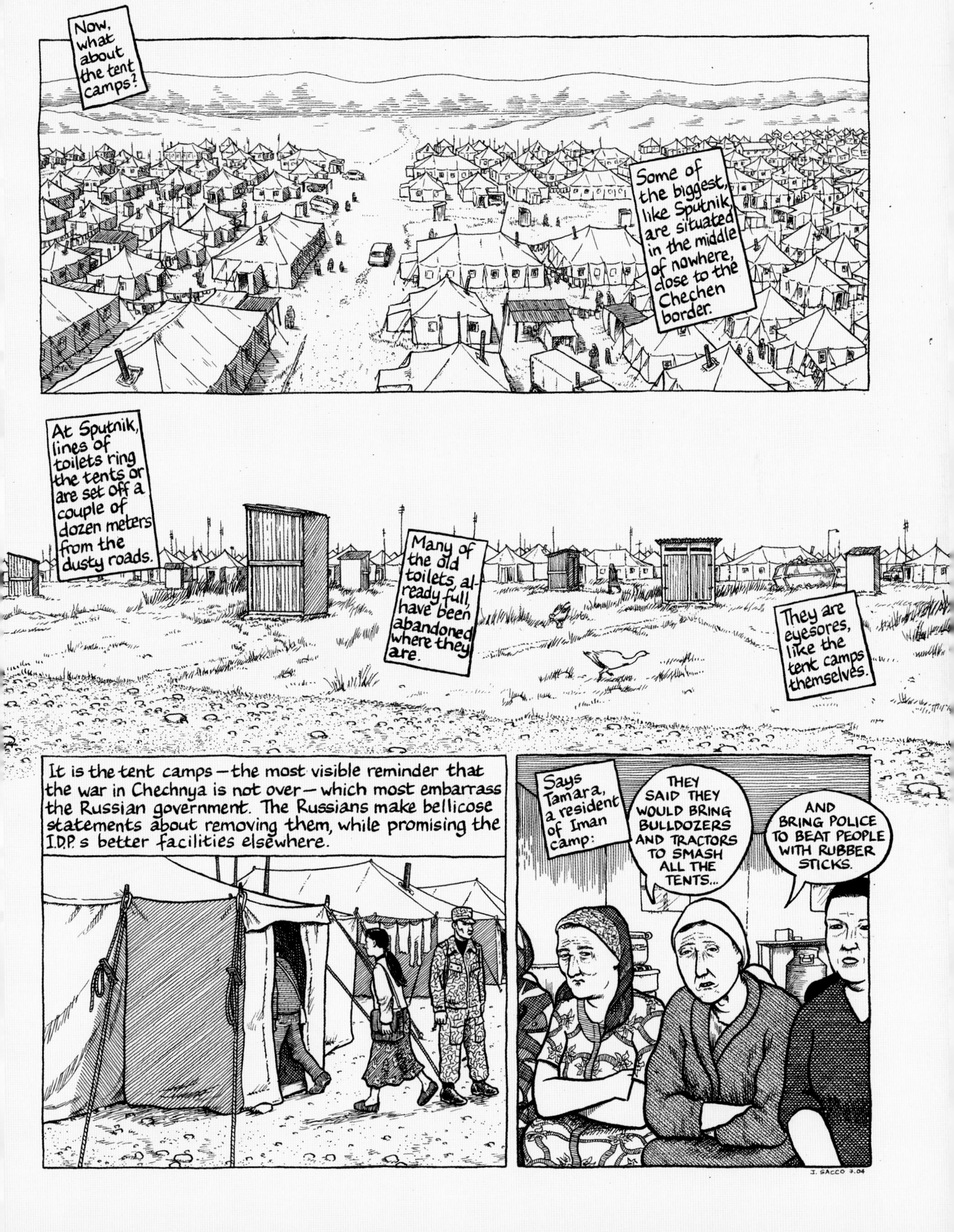
Now, what about the tent camps?
Some of the biggest, like Sputnik, are situated in the middle of nowhere, close to the Chechen border.
At Sputnik, lines of toilets ring the tents or are set off a couple of dozen meters from the dusty roads.
Many of the old toilets, already full, have been abandoned where they are.
They are eyesores, like the tent camps themselves.
It is the tent camps—the most visible reminder that the war in Chechnya is not over—which most embarrass the Russian government. The Russians make bellicose statements about removing them, while promising the I.D.P.s better facilities elsewhere.
Says Tamara, a resident of Iman camp:
THEY SAID THEY WOULD BRING BULLDOZERS AND TRACTORS TO SMASH ALL THE TENTS...
AND BRING POLICE TO BEAT PEOPLE WITH RUBBER STICKS.
J. SACCO 7.04

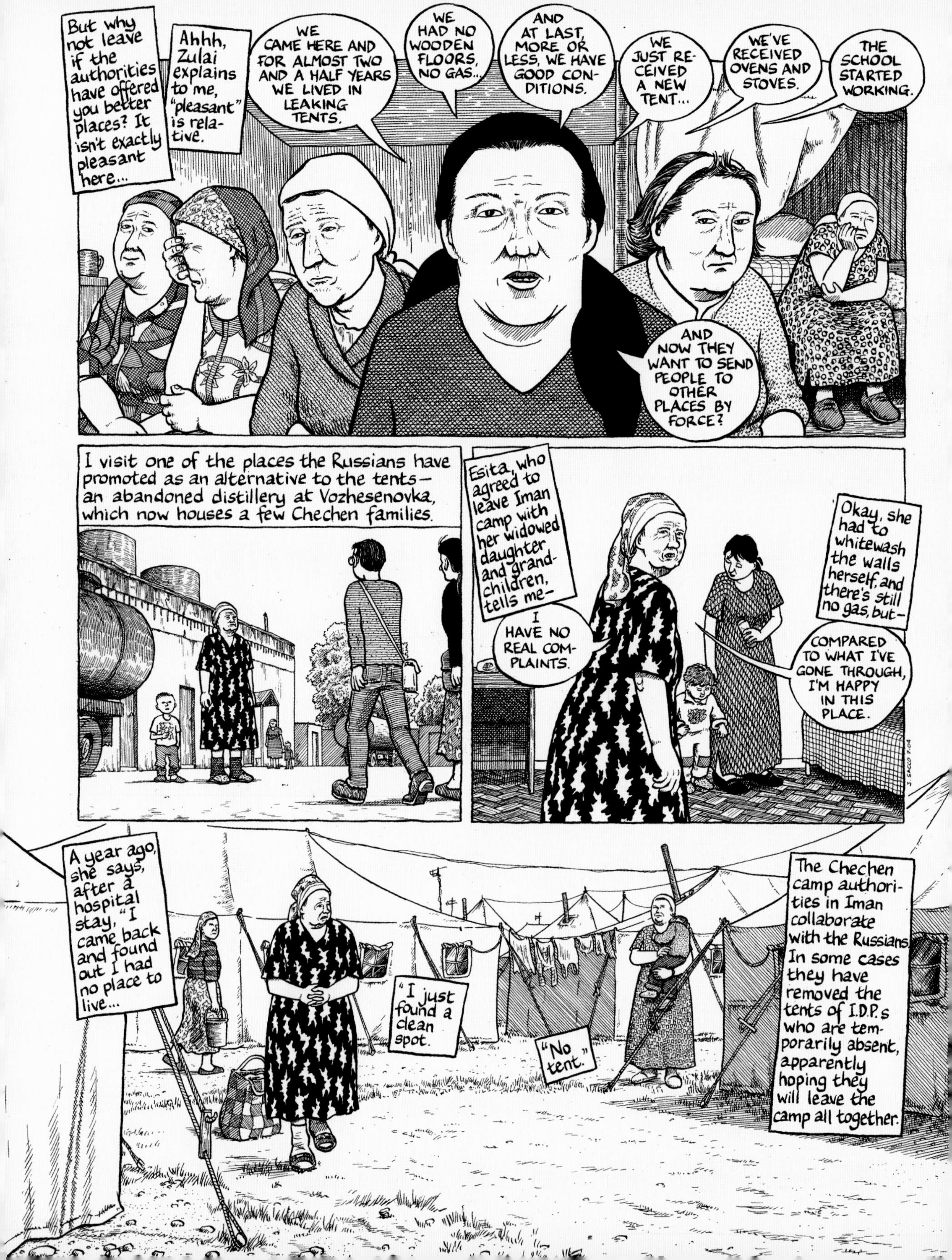
But why not leave if the authorities have offered you better places? It isn't exactly pleasant here...
Ahhh, Zulai explains to me, "pleasant" is relative.
WE CAME HERE AND FOR ALMOST TWO AND A HALF YEARS WE LIVED IN LEAKING TENTS.
WE HAD NO WOODEN FLOORS, NO GAS...
AND AT LAST, MORE OR LESS, WE HAVE GOOD CONDITIONS.
WE JUST RECEIVED A NEW TENT...
WE'VE RECEIVED OVENS AND STOVES.
THE SCHOOL STARTED WORKING.
AND NOW THEY WANT TO SEND PEOPLE TO OTHER PLACES BY FORCE?
I visit one of the places the Russians have promoted as an alternative to the tents—an abandoned distillery at Vozhesenovka, which now houses a few Chechen families.
Esita, who agreed to leave Iman camp with her widowed daughter and grandchildren, tells me—
I HAVE NO REAL COMPLAINTS.
Okay, she had to whitewash the walls herself, and there's still no gas, but—
COMPARED TO WHAT I'VE GONE THROUGH, I'M HAPPY IN THIS PLACE.
A year ago, she says, after a hospital stay, "I came back and found out I had no place to live...
"I just found a clean spot.
"No tent."
The Chechen camp authorities in Iman collaborate with the Russians. In some cases they have removed the tents of I.D.P.s who are temporarily absent, apparently hoping they will leave the camp all together.

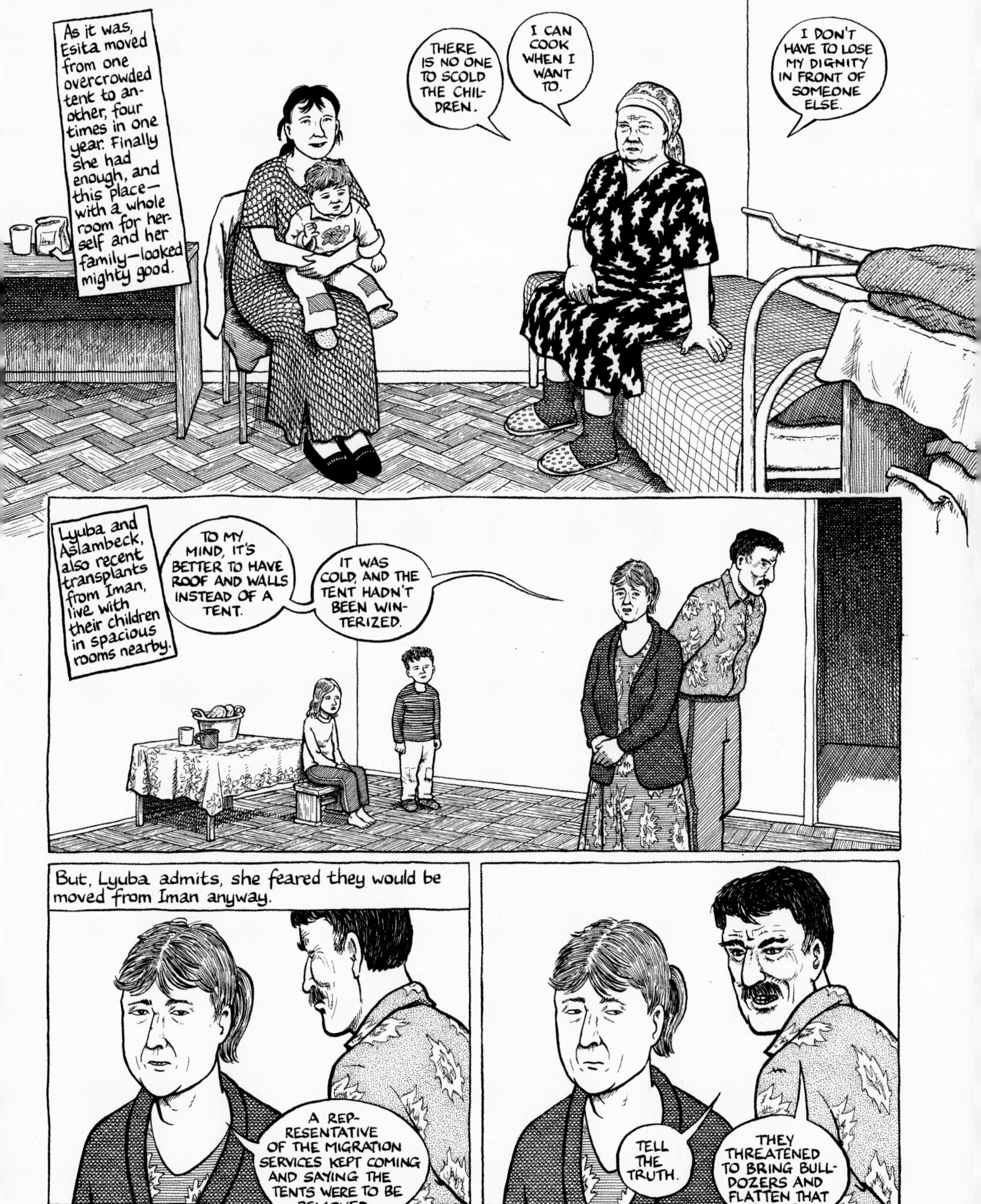
As it was, Esita moved from one overcrowded tent to another, four times in one year. Finally she had enough, and this place—with a whole room for herself and her family—looked mighty good.
THERE IS NO ONE TO SCOLD THE CHILDREN.
I CAN COOK WHEN I WANT TO.
I DON'T HAVE TO LOSE MY DIGNITY IN FRONT OF SOMEONE ELSE.
Lyuba and Aslambeck, also recent transplants from Iman, live with their children in spacious rooms nearby.
TO MY MIND, IT'S BETTER TO HAVE ROOF AND WALLS INSTEAD OF A TENT.
IT WAS COLD, AND THE TENT HADN'T BEEN WINTERIZED.
But, Lyuba admits, she feared they would be moved from Iman anyway.
A REPRESENTATIVE OF THE MIGRATION SERVICES KEPT COMING AND SAYING THE TENTS WERE TO BE REMOVED.
TELL THE TRUTH.
THEY THREATENED TO BRING BULLDOZERS AND FLATTEN THAT PLACE.
J. SACCO 7.04

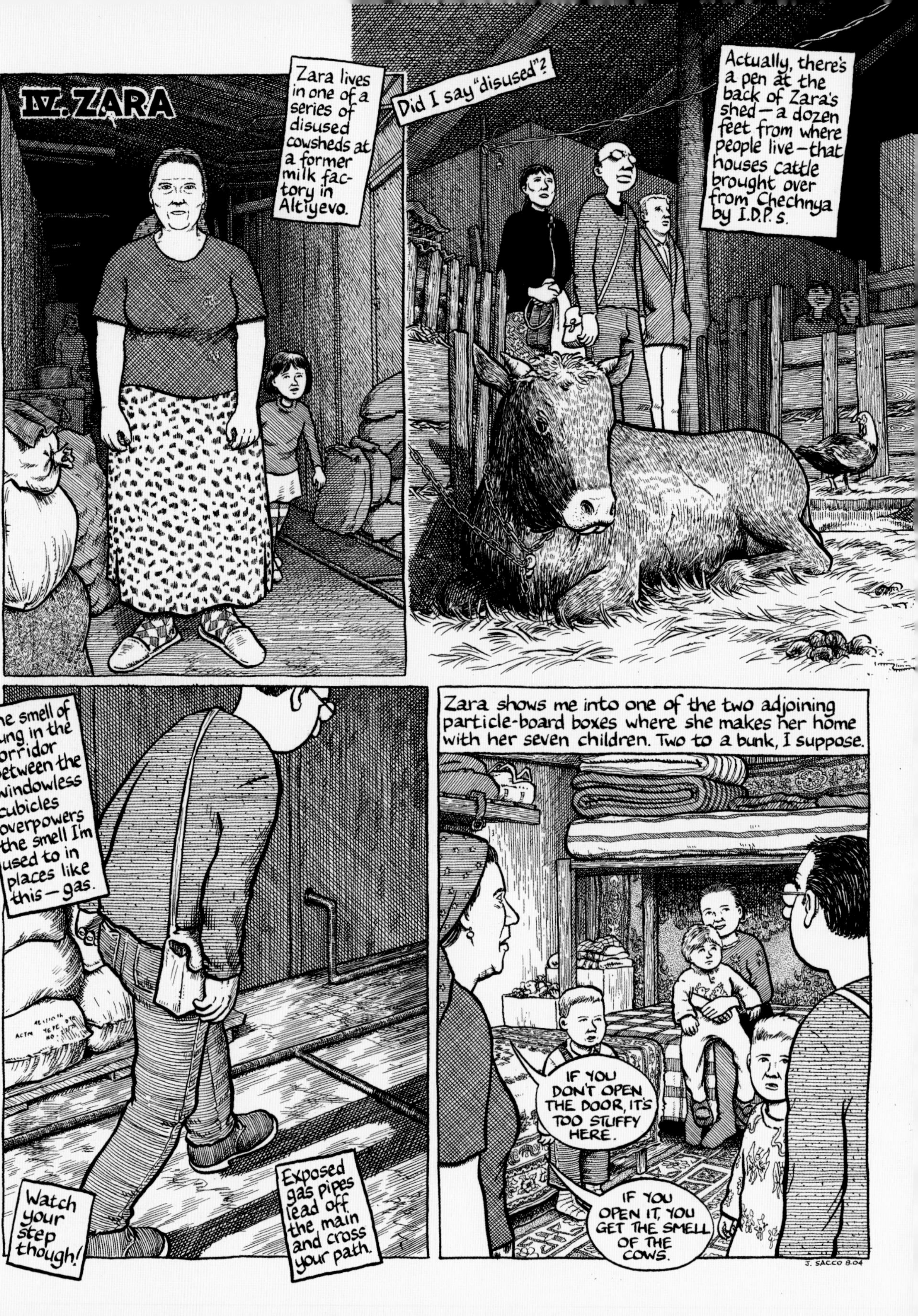
IV. ZARA
Zara lives in one of a series of disused cowsheds at a former milk factory in Altiyevo.
Did I say "disused"?
Actually, there's a pen at the back of Zara's shed—a dozen feet from where people live—that houses cattle brought over from Chechnya by I.D.P.s.
The smell of dung in the corridor between the windowless cubicles overpowers the smell I'm used to in places like this—gas.
Watch your step though!
Exposed gas pipes lead off the main and cross your path.
Zara shows me into one of the two adjoining particle-board boxes where she makes her home with her seven children. Two to a bunk, I suppose.
IF YOU DON'T OPEN THE DOOR, IT'S TOO STUFFY HERE.
IF YOU OPEN IT, YOU GET THE SMELL OF THE COWS.
J. SACCO 8.04

It's stuffy all right, but as cheery as a room in a cowshed can get. She's hung up carpets on the wall.

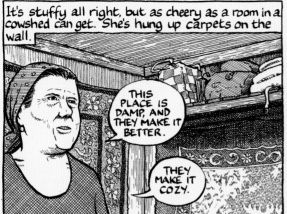

THIS PLACE IS DAMP, AND THEY MAKE IT BETTER.

THEY MAKE IT COZY.

Zara bought these rooms for 4,000 rubles from the previous owner, who built them himself from donated material and charged her for his labor.

She's just paid another 3,000 on a room for her husband, who only escaped from Chechnya last month, and his two nephews, who were orphaned in the first war.

His name is Issa.

He is watchful but sits passively while Zara does the talking.

He has been tortured, she says.

Detained for six months.

Tortured.

As if on cue, he hikes up his trouser leg. The Russians shot him, you see. He was sitting with his hands on his head and they put a bullet through his ankle.

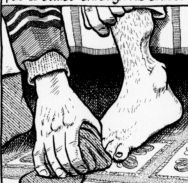

He yanks up his pullover.

You see the welts?

They heated up a knife and cut him with it over and over.

HE ALMOST WENT INSANE.

HE DIDN'T RECOGNIZE HIS OWN FAMILY WHEN HE WAS RELEASED.

HE BEAT THE CHILDREN.

HE BEAT OUR OWN DAUGHTER SO SEVERELY THAT SHE ALSO HAS MENTAL PROBLEMS.

ONCE HE TIED MY HANDS TOGETHER AND MY FEET TOGETHER AND WAS GOING TO SLAUGHTER ME WITH A KNIFE.

J. SACCO 8·04

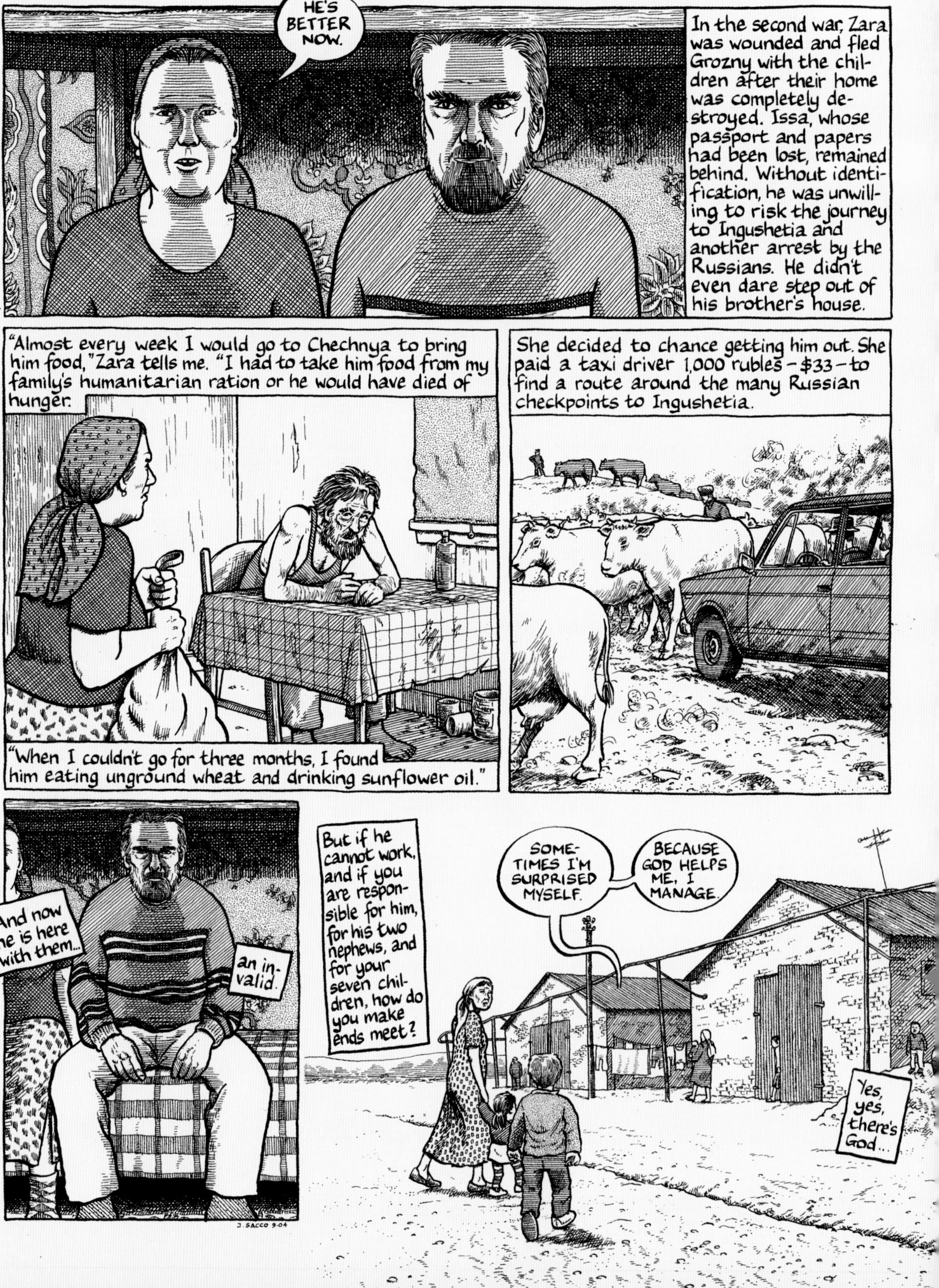
HE'S BETTER NOW.
In the second war, Zara was wounded and fled Grozny with the children after their home was completely destroyed. Issa, whose passport and papers had been lost, remained behind. Without identification, he was unwilling to risk the journey to Ingushetia and another arrest by the Russians. He didn't even dare step out of his brother's house.
"Almost every week I would go to Chechnya to bring him food," Zara tells me. "I had to take him food from my family's humanitarian ration or he would have died of hunger.
"When I couldn't go for three months, I found him eating unground wheat and drinking sunflower oil."
She decided to chance getting him out. She paid a taxi driver 1,000 rubles—$33—to find a route around the many Russian checkpoints to Ingushetia.
And now he is here with them...
an invalid.
But if he cannot work, and if you are responsible for him, for his two nephews, and for your seven children, how do you make ends meet?
SOMETIMES I'M SURPRISED MYSELF.
BECAUSE GOD HELPS ME, I MANAGE.
Yes, yes, there's God...
J. SACCO 9.04

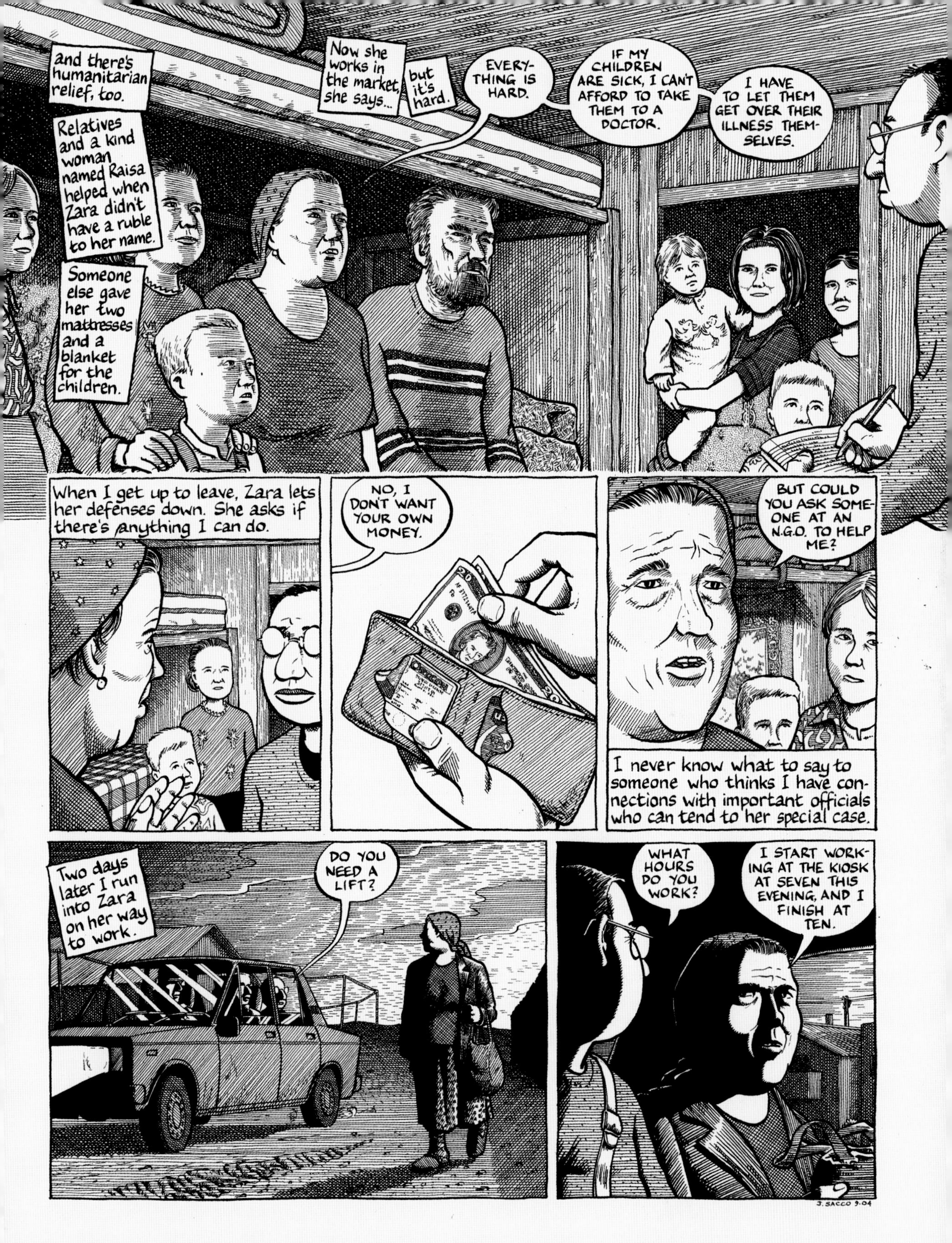

and there's humanitarian relief, too.
Relatives and a kind woman named Raisa helped when Zara didn't have a ruble to her name.
Someone else gave her two mattresses and a blanket for the children.
Now she works in the market, she says...
but it's hard.
EVERYTHING IS HARD.
IF MY CHILDREN ARE SICK, I CAN'T AFFORD TO TAKE THEM TO A DOCTOR.
I HAVE TO LET THEM GET OVER THEIR ILLNESS THEMSELVES.
When I get up to leave, Zara lets her defenses down. She asks if there's anything I can do.
NO, I DON'T WANT YOUR OWN MONEY.
BUT COULD YOU ASK SOMEONE AT AN N.G.O. TO HELP ME?
I never know what to say to someone who thinks I have connections with important officials who can tend to her special case.
Two days later I run into Zara on her way to work.
DO YOU NEED A LIFT?
WHAT HOURS DO YOU WORK?
I START WORKING AT THE KIOSK AT SEVEN THIS EVENING, AND I FINISH AT TEN.
J. SACCO 9.04

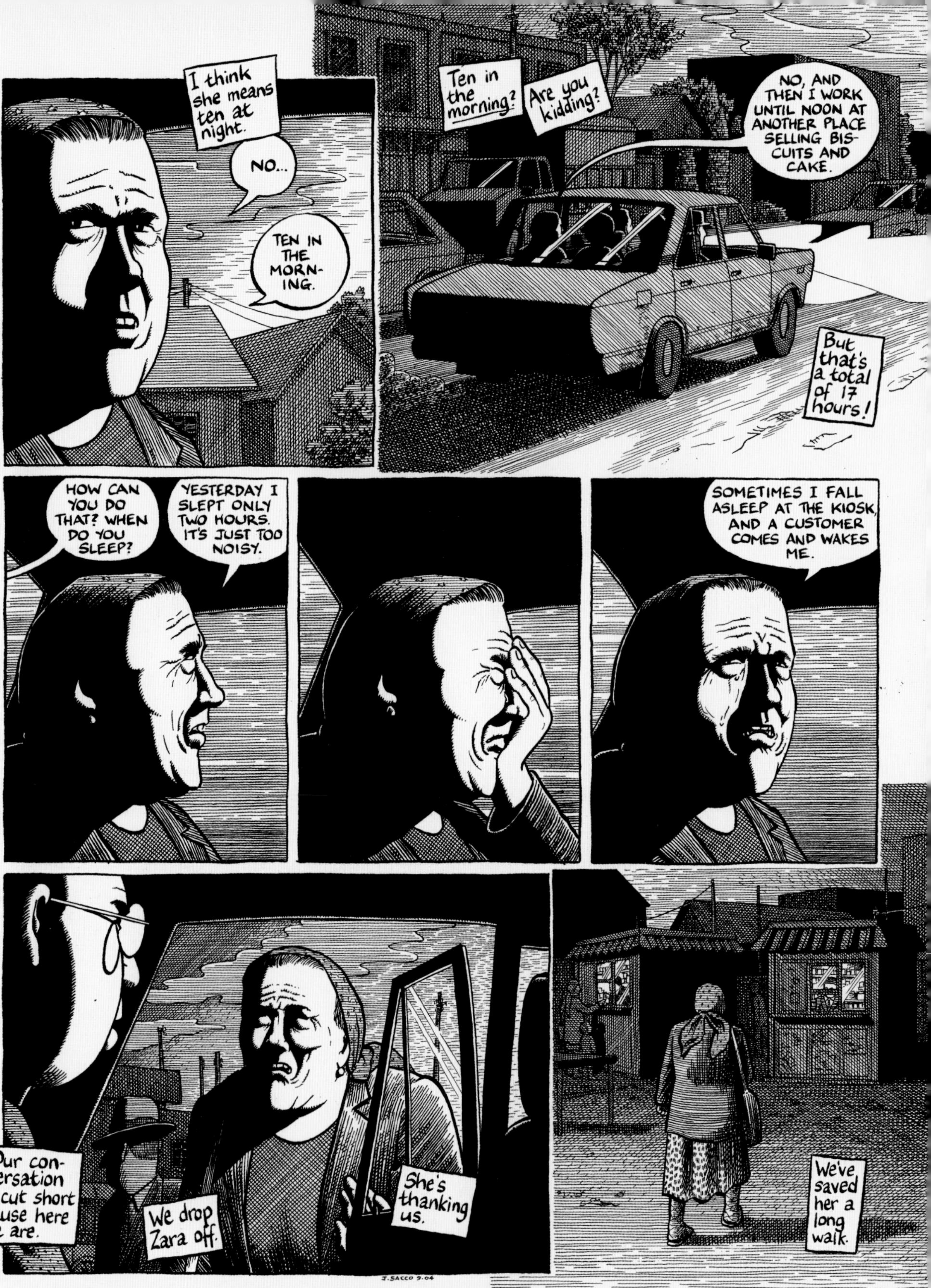

I think she means ten at night.
NO...
TEN IN THE MORN-ING.
Ten in the morning?
Are you kidding?
NO, AND THEN I WORK UNTIL NOON AT ANOTHER PLACE SELLING BIS-CUITS AND CAKE.
But that's a total of 17 hours!
HOW CAN YOU DO THAT? WHEN DO YOU SLEEP?
YESTERDAY I SLEPT ONLY TWO HOURS. IT'S JUST TOO NOISY.
SOMETIMES I FALL ASLEEP AT THE KIOSK, AND A CUSTOMER COMES AND WAKES ME.
Our con-versation is cut short 'cause here we are.
We drop Zara off.
She's thanking us.
We've saved her a long walk.
J. SACCO 9.04

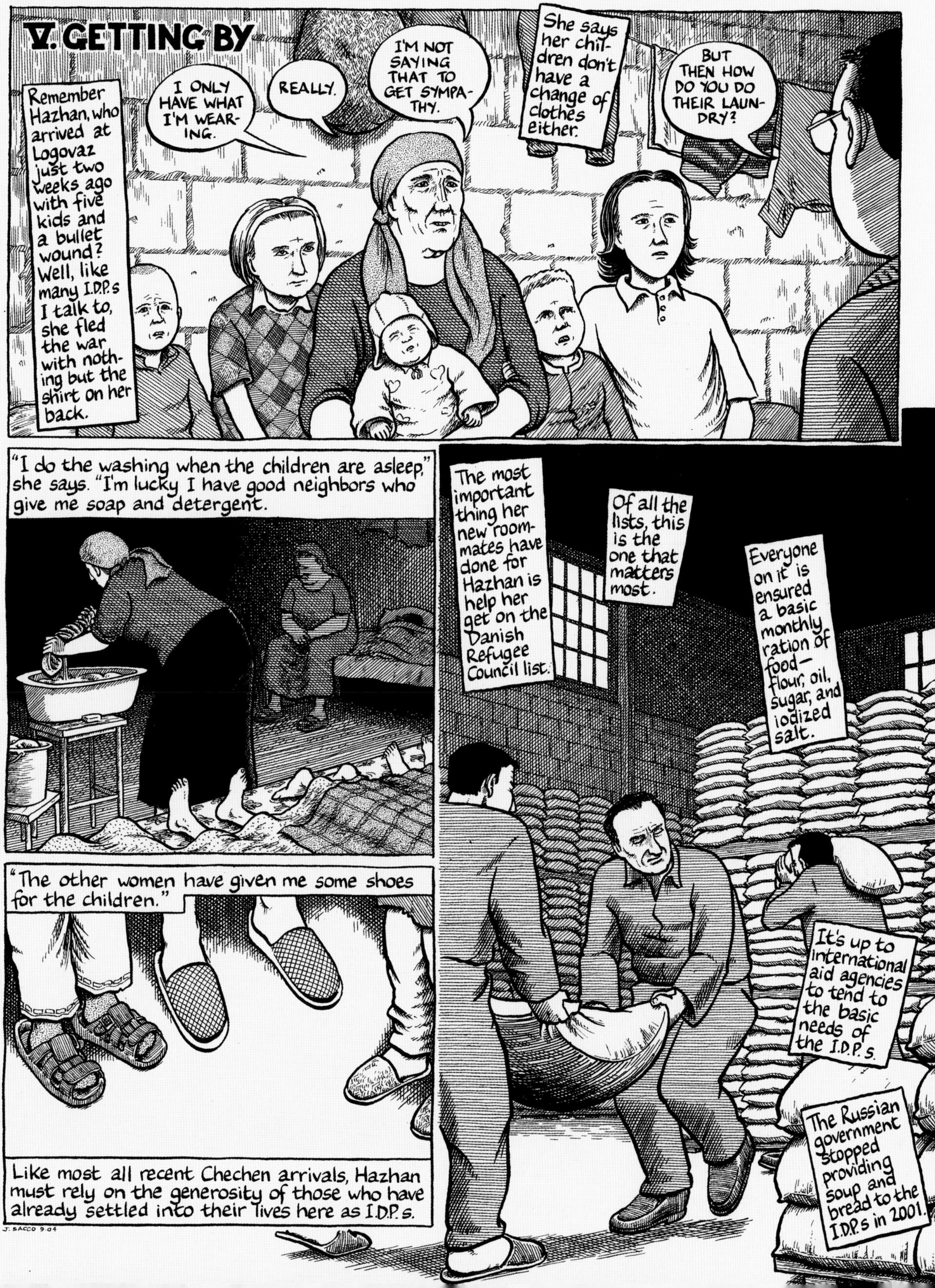

V. GETTING BY
Remember Hazhan, who arrived at Logovaz just two weeks ago with five kids and a bullet wound? Well, like many I.D.P.s I talk to, she fled the war with nothing but the shirt on her back.
I ONLY HAVE WHAT I'M WEARING.
REALLY.
I'M NOT SAYING THAT TO GET SYMPATHY.
She says her children don't have a change of clothes either.
BUT THEN HOW DO YOU DO THEIR LAUNDRY?
"I do the washing when the children are asleep," she says. "I'm lucky I have good neighbors who give me soap and detergent.
"The other women have given me some shoes for the children."
Like most all recent Chechen arrivals, Hazhan must rely on the generosity of those who have already settled into their lives here as I.D.P.s.
The most important thing her new roommates have done for Hazhan is help her get on the Danish Refugee Council list.
Of all the lists, this is the one that matters most.
Everyone on it is ensured a basic monthly ration of food—flour, oil, sugar, and iodized salt.
It's up to international aid agencies to tend to the basic needs of the I.D.P.s.
The Russian government stopped providing soup and bread to the I.D.P.s in 2001.
J. SACCO 9.04

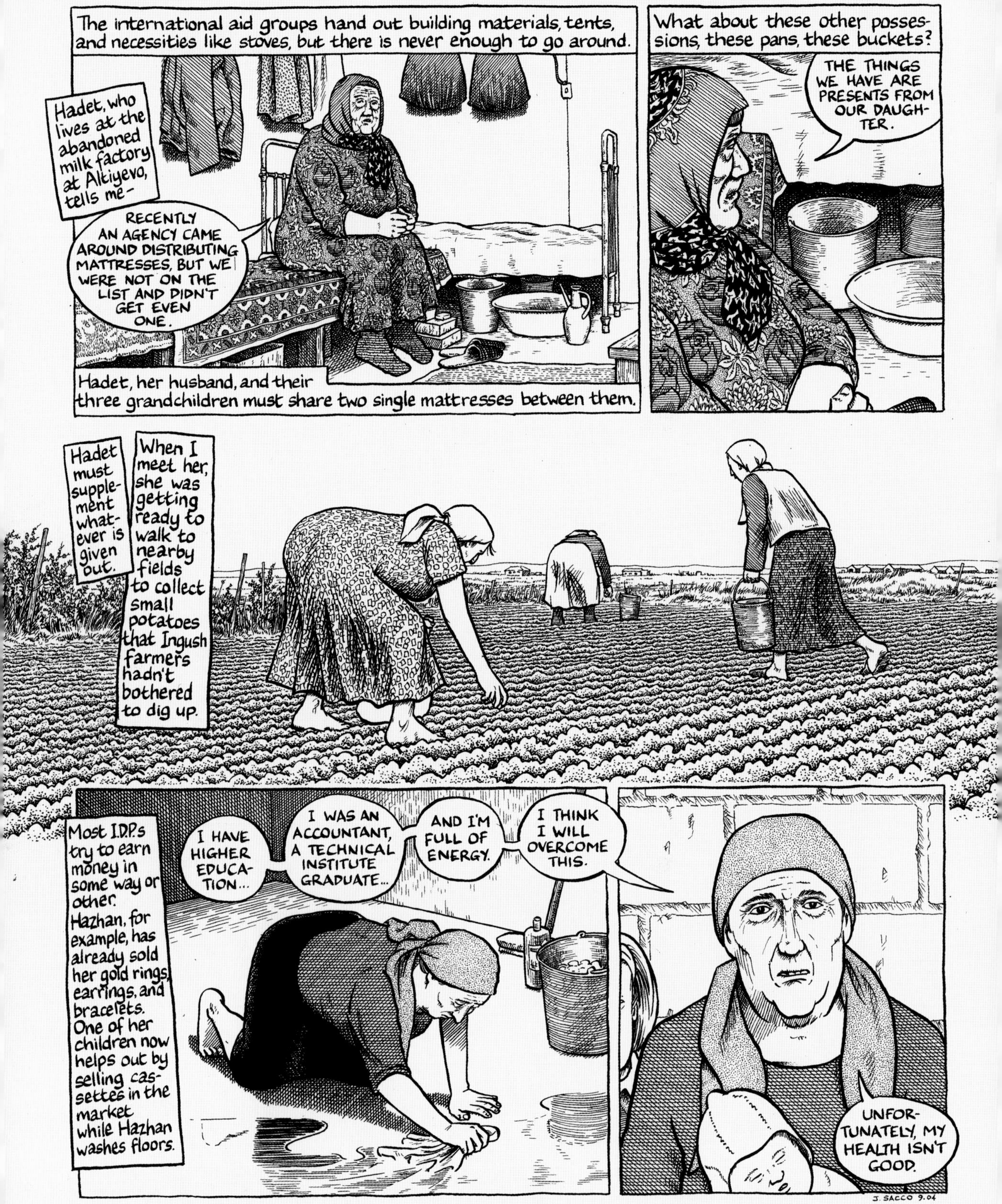

The international aid groups hand out building materials, tents, and necessities like stoves, but there is never enough to go around.
Hadet, who lives at the abandoned milk factory at Altiyevo, tells me-
RECENTLY AN AGENCY CAME AROUND DISTRIBUTING MATTRESSES, BUT WE WERE NOT ON THE LIST AND DIDN'T GET EVEN ONE.
Hadet, her husband, and their three grandchildren must share two single mattresses between them.
What about these other possessions, these pans, these buckets?
THE THINGS WE HAVE ARE PRESENTS FROM OUR DAUGHTER.
Hadet must supplement whatever is given out.
When I meet her, she was getting ready to walk to nearby fields to collect small potatoes that Ingush farmers hadn't bothered to dig up.
Most I.D.P.s try to earn money in some way or other. Hazhan, for example, has already sold her gold rings, earrings, and bracelets. One of her children now helps out by selling cassettes in the market while Hazhan washes floors.
I HAVE HIGHER EDUCATION...
I WAS AN ACCOUNTANT, A TECHNICAL INSTITUTE GRADUATE...
AND I'M FULL OF ENERGY.
I THINK I WILL OVERCOME THIS.
UNFORTUNATELY, MY HEALTH ISN'T GOOD.
J. SACCO 9.04

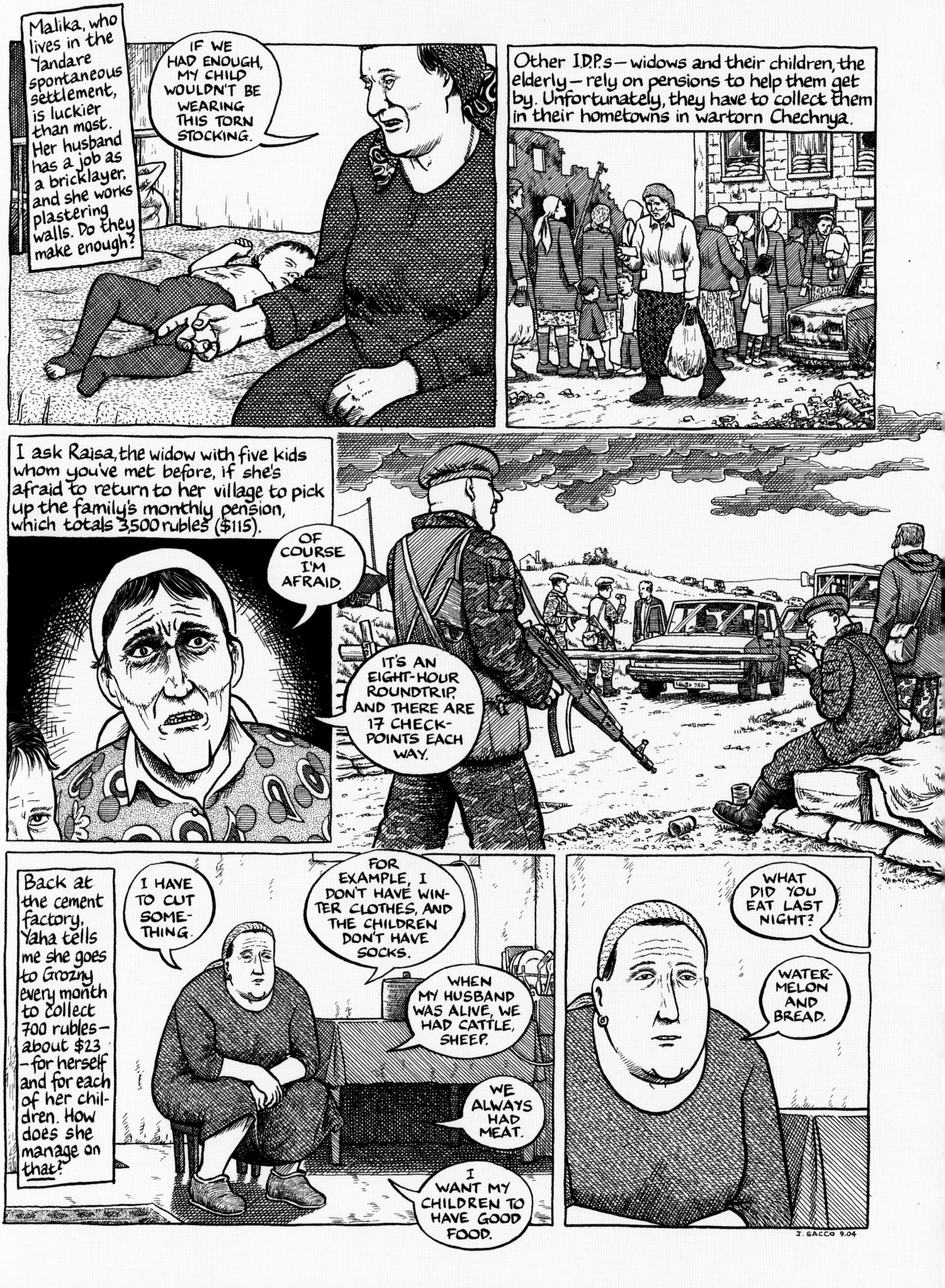
Malika, who lives in the Yandare spontaneous settlement, is luckier than most. Her husband has a job as a bricklayer, and she works plastering walls. Do they make enough?
IF WE HAD ENOUGH, MY CHILD WOULDN'T BE WEARING THIS TORN STOCKING.
Other I.D.P.s — widows and their children, the elderly — rely on pensions to help them get by. Unfortunately, they have to collect them in their hometowns in wartorn Chechnya.
I ask Raisa, the widow with five kids whom you've met before, if she's afraid to return to her village to pick up the family's monthly pension, which totals 3,500 rubles ($115).
OF COURSE I'M AFRAID.
IT'S AN EIGHT-HOUR ROUNDTRIP, AND THERE ARE 17 CHECK-POINTS EACH WAY.
Back at the cement factory, Yaha tells me she goes to Grozny every month to collect 700 rubles — about $23 — for herself and for each of her children. How does she manage on that?
I HAVE TO CUT SOME-THING.
FOR EXAMPLE, I DON'T HAVE WIN-TER CLOTHES, AND THE CHILDREN DON'T HAVE SOCKS.
WHEN MY HUSBAND WAS ALIVE, WE HAD CATTLE, SHEEP.
WE ALWAYS HAD MEAT.
I WANT MY CHILDREN TO HAVE GOOD FOOD.
WHAT DID YOU EAT LAST NIGHT?
WATER-MELON AND BREAD.
J. SACCO 9.04

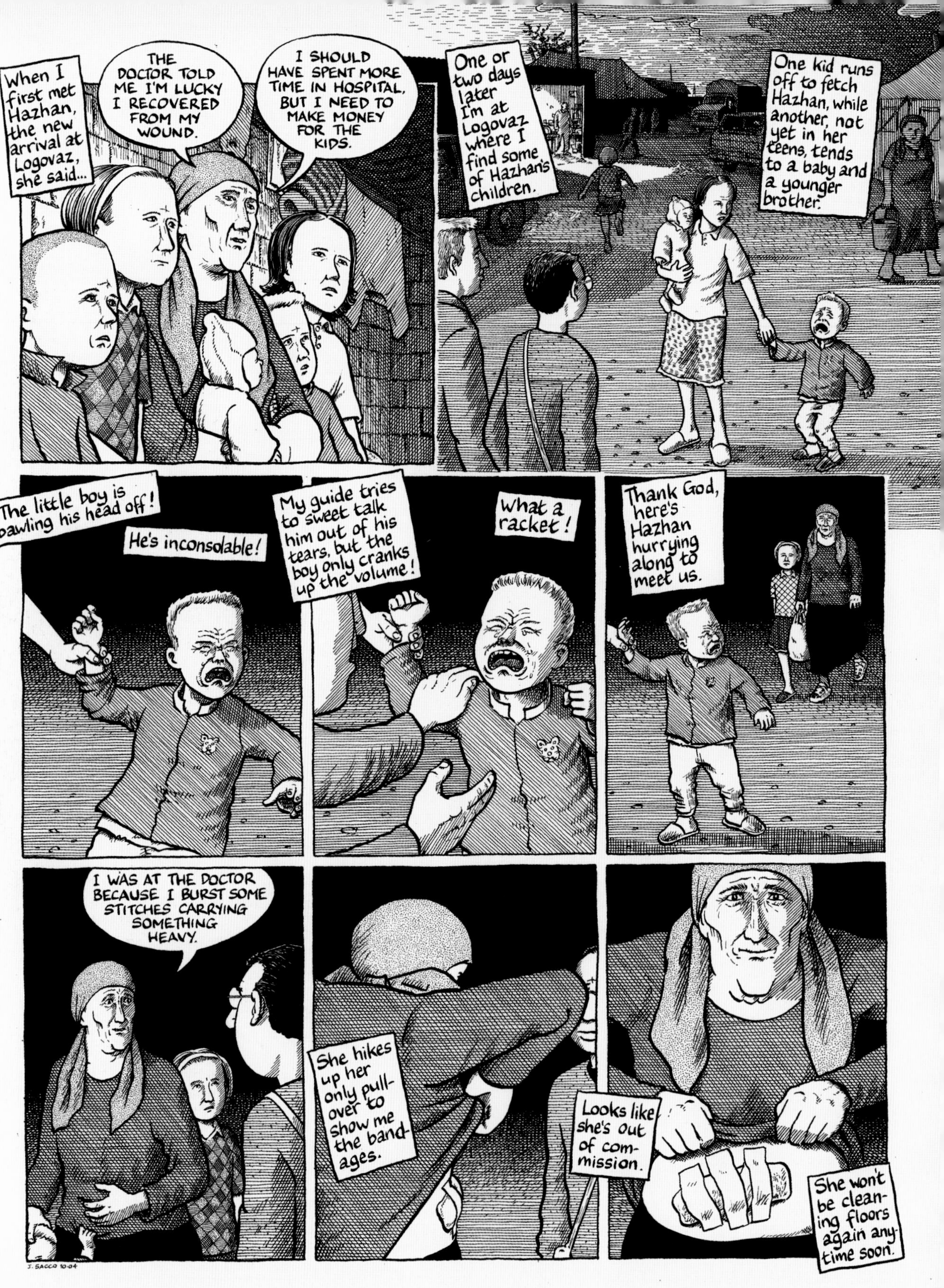
When I first met Hazhan, the new arrival at Logovaz, she said...
THE DOCTOR TOLD ME I'M LUCKY I RECOVERED FROM MY WOUND.
I SHOULD HAVE SPENT MORE TIME IN HOSPITAL, BUT I NEED TO MAKE MONEY FOR THE KIDS.
One or two days later I'm at Logovaz where I find some of Hazhan's children.
One kid runs off to fetch Hazhan, while another, not yet in her teens, tends to a baby and a younger brother.
The little boy is bawling his head off!
He's inconsolable!
My guide tries to sweet talk him out of his tears, but the boy only cranks up the volume!
What a racket!
Thank God, here's Hazhan hurrying along to meet us.
I WAS AT THE DOCTOR BECAUSE I BURST SOME STITCHES CARRYING SOMETHING HEAVY.
She hikes up her only pull-over to show me the band-ages.
Looks like she's out of com-mission.
She won't be clean-ing floors again any-time soon.
J. SACCO 10-04

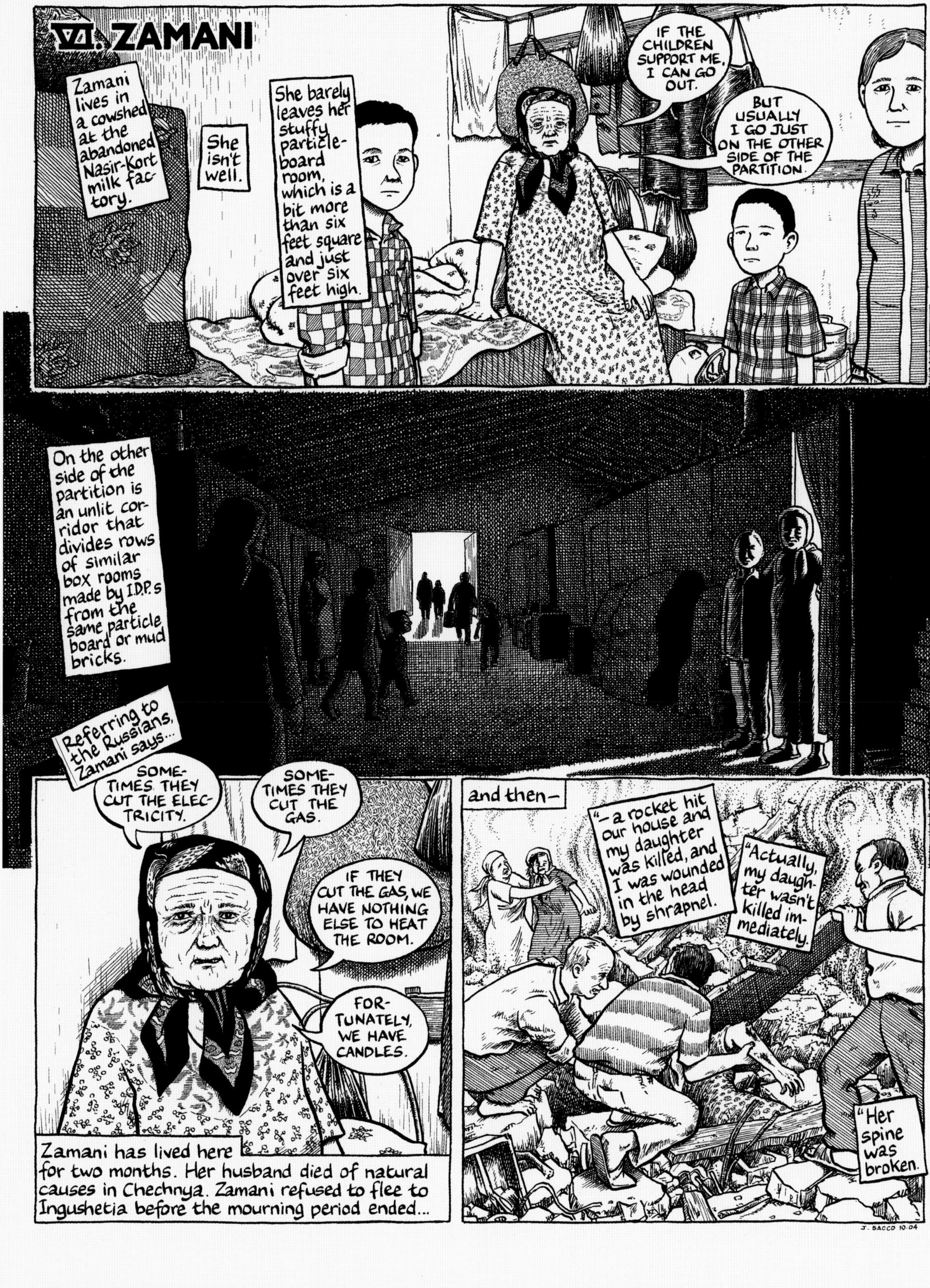
VI. ZAMANI
Zamani lives in a cowshed at the abandoned Nasir-Kort milk factory.
She isn't well.
She barely leaves her stuffy particle-board room, which is a bit more than six feet square and just over six feet high.
IF THE CHILDREN SUPPORT ME, I CAN GO OUT.
BUT USUALLY I GO JUST ON THE OTHER SIDE OF THE PARTITION.
On the other side of the partition is an unlit corridor that divides rows of similar box rooms made by I.D.P.s from the same particle board or mud bricks.
Referring to the Russians, Zamani says...
SOMETIMES THEY CUT THE ELECTRICITY.
SOMETIMES THEY CUT THE GAS.
IF THEY CUT THE GAS, WE HAVE NOTHING ELSE TO HEAT THE ROOM.
FORTUNATELY, WE HAVE CANDLES.
Zamani has lived here for two months. Her husband died of natural causes in Chechnya. Zamani refused to flee to Ingushetia before the mourning period ended...
and then–
"–a rocket hit our house and my daughter was killed, and I was wounded in the head by shrapnel.
"Actually, my daughter wasn't killed immediately.
"Her spine was broken.
J. SACCO 10.04

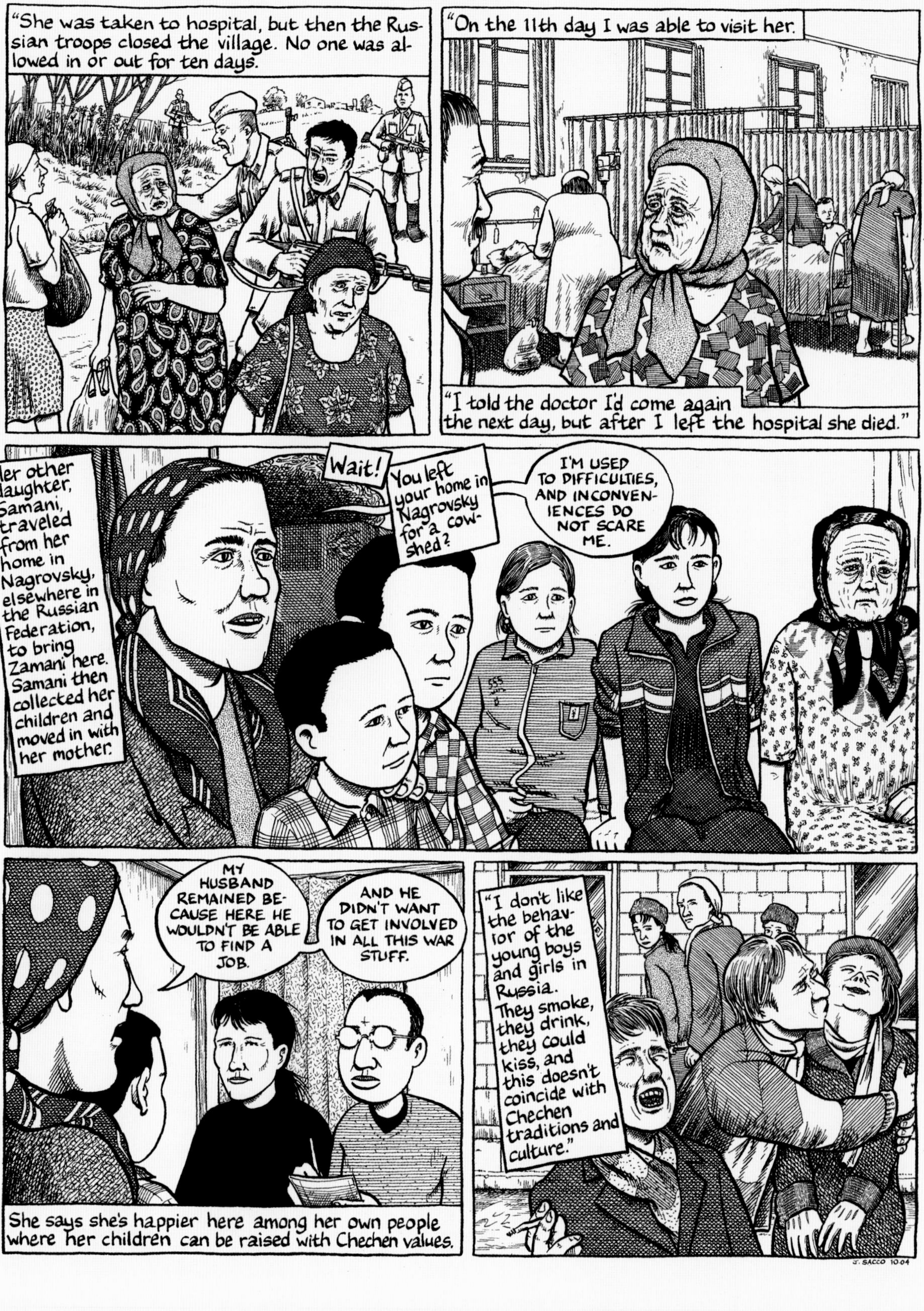
"She was taken to hospital, but then the Russian troops closed the village. No one was allowed in or out for ten days.
"On the 11th day I was able to visit her.
"I told the doctor I'd come again the next day, but after I left the hospital she died."
Her other daughter, Samani, traveled from her home in Nagrovsky, elsewhere in the Russian Federation, to bring Zamani here. Samani then collected her children and moved in with her mother.
Wait!
You left your home in Nagrovsky for a cow-shed?
I'M USED TO DIFFICULTIES, AND INCONVENIENCES DO NOT SCARE ME.
MY HUSBAND REMAINED BECAUSE HERE HE WOULDN'T BE ABLE TO FIND A JOB.
AND HE DIDN'T WANT TO GET INVOLVED IN ALL THIS WAR STUFF.
She says she's happier here among her own people where her children can be raised with Chechen values.
"I don't like the behavior of the young boys and girls in Russia. They smoke, they drink, they could kiss, and this doesn't coincide with Chechen traditions and culture."
J. SACCO 10.04

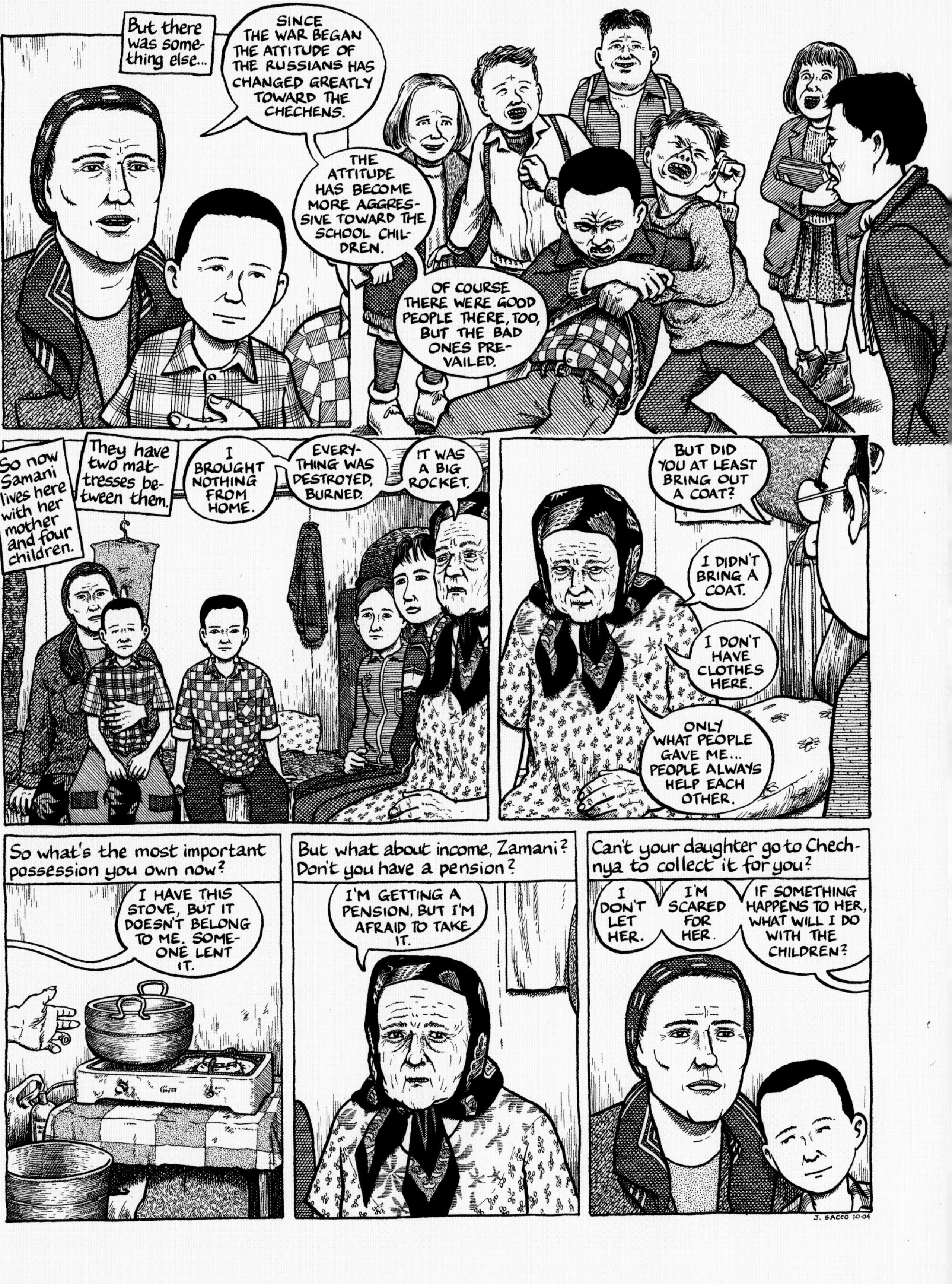
But there was something else...
SINCE THE WAR BEGAN THE ATTITUDE OF THE RUSSIANS HAS CHANGED GREATLY TOWARD THE CHECHENS.
THE ATTITUDE HAS BECOME MORE AGGRESSIVE TOWARD THE SCHOOL CHILDREN.
OF COURSE THERE WERE GOOD PEOPLE THERE, TOO, BUT THE BAD ONES PREVAILED.
So now Samani lives here with her mother and four children.
They have two mattresses between them.
I BROUGHT NOTHING FROM HOME.
EVERYTHING WAS DESTROYED, BURNED.
IT WAS A BIG ROCKET.
BUT DID YOU AT LEAST BRING OUT A COAT?
I DIDN'T BRING A COAT.
I DON'T HAVE CLOTHES HERE.
ONLY WHAT PEOPLE GAVE ME... PEOPLE ALWAYS HELP EACH OTHER.
So what's the most important possession you own now?
I HAVE THIS STOVE, BUT IT DOESN'T BELONG TO ME. SOMEONE LENT IT.
But what about income, Zamani? Don't you have a pension?
I'M GETTING A PENSION, BUT I'M AFRAID TO TAKE IT.
Can't your daughter go to Chechnya to collect it for you?
I DON'T LET HER.
I'M SCARED FOR HER.
IF SOMETHING HAPPENS TO HER, WHAT WILL I DO WITH THE CHILDREN?
J. SACCO 10·04

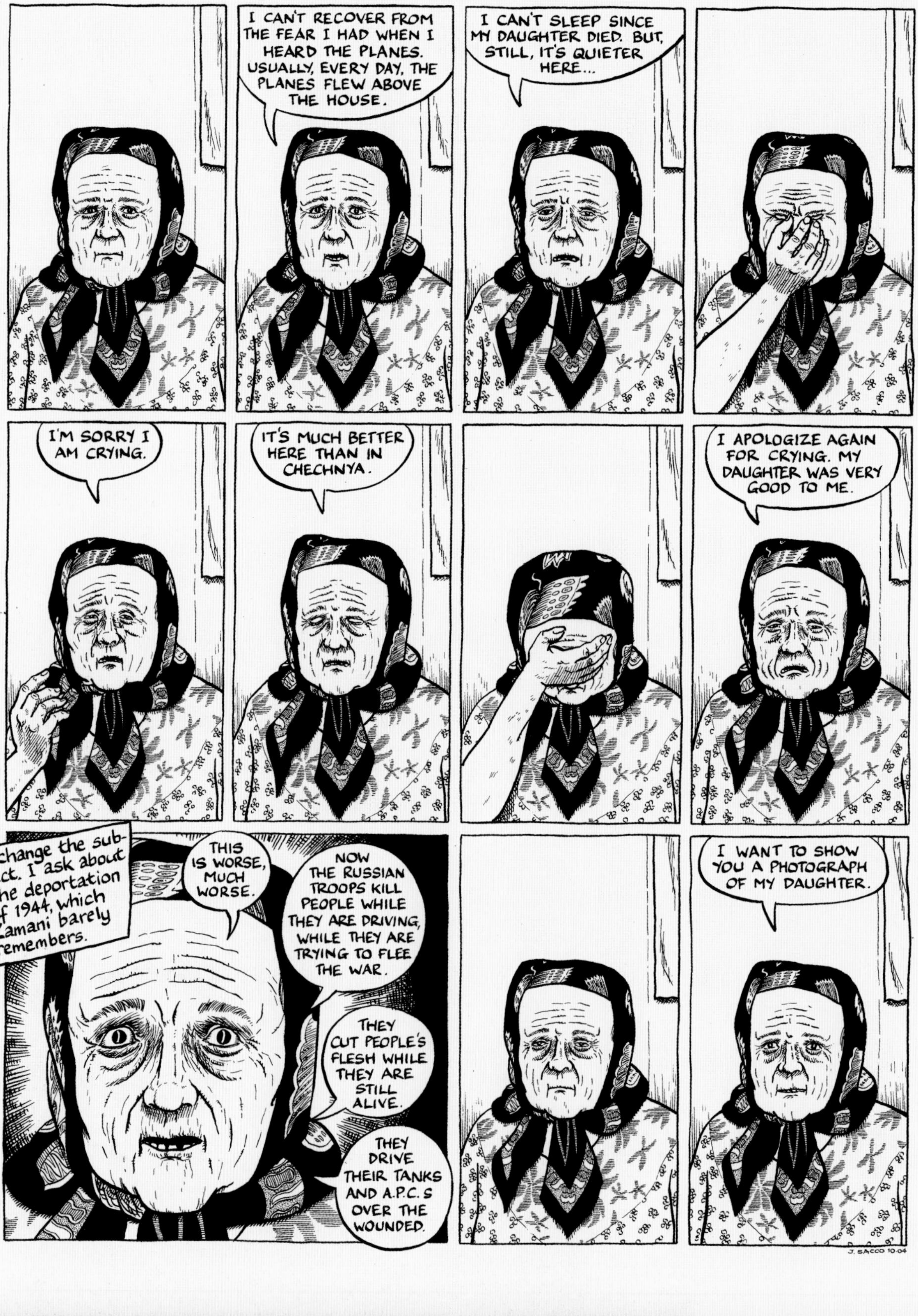
I CAN'T RECOVER FROM THE FEAR I HAD WHEN I HEARD THE PLANES. USUALLY, EVERY DAY, THE PLANES FLEW ABOVE THE HOUSE.
I CAN'T SLEEP SINCE MY DAUGHTER DIED. BUT, STILL, IT'S QUIETER HERE...
I'M SORRY I AM CRYING.
IT'S MUCH BETTER HERE THAN IN CHECHNYA.
I APOLOGIZE AGAIN FOR CRYING. MY DAUGHTER WAS VERY GOOD TO ME.
I change the subject. I ask about the deportation of 1944, which Zamani barely remembers.
THIS IS WORSE, MUCH WORSE.
NOW THE RUSSIAN TROOPS KILL PEOPLE WHILE THEY ARE DRIVING, WHILE THEY ARE TRYING TO FLEE THE WAR.
THEY CUT PEOPLE'S FLESH WHILE THEY ARE STILL ALIVE.
THEY DRIVE THEIR TANKS AND A.P.C.S OVER THE WOUNDED.
I WANT TO SHOW YOU A PHOTOGRAPH OF MY DAUGHTER.
J. SACCO 10-04

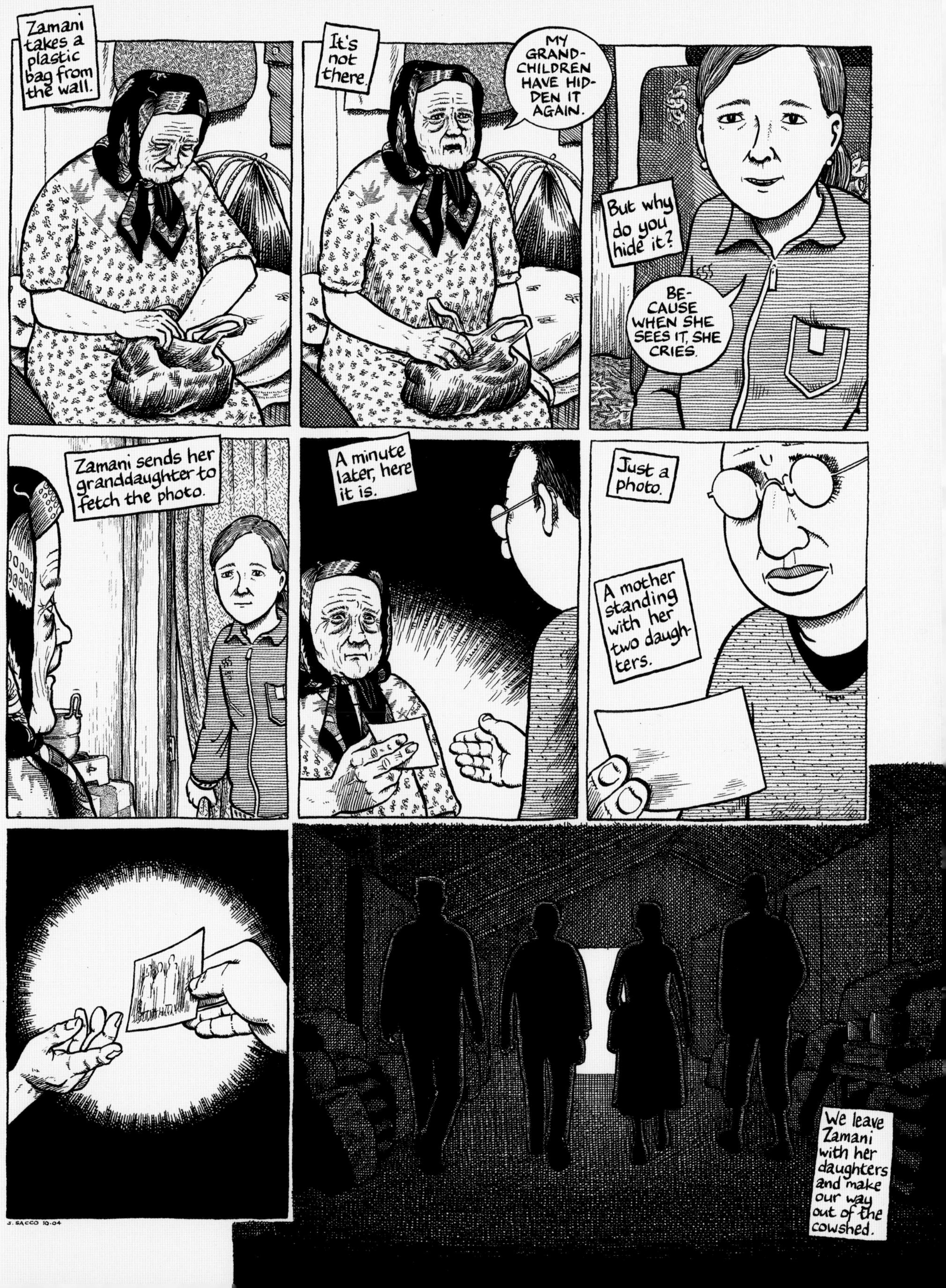

Zamani takes a plastic bag from the wall.
It's not there.
MY GRAND-CHILDREN HAVE HID-DEN IT AGAIN.
But why do you hide it?
BE-CAUSE WHEN SHE SEES IT, SHE CRIES.
Zamani sends her granddaughter to fetch the photo.
A minute later, here it is.
Just a photo.
A mother standing with her two daugh-ters.
We leave Zamani with her daughters and make our way out of the cowshed.
J. SACCO 10.04

Moscow. The Ukraina Hotel.

Outside, snow hisses at my window. I am thinking about her mouth. When Tamara spoke, her mouth formed perfect O's so you could see everything down her throat. Her mouth was like a canal, her teeth like small buildings about to be demolished. We sat in the offices of Memorial, a human rights organization based in Moscow. It was my last day in Russia.

Today, Tamara said, she had just returned from Grozny, where she had been arrested and detained. Her interrogator, she said, kept repeating the same words. "I am Vladimir Putin's son. Do you know that? Putin's son." She showed me her arm, as if to offer her bruises as proof of her ordeal. I didn't want to tell her that I couldn't see anything.

It all started with her cheap camera, one of those disposables you can buy in the Rite Aid checkout line. When the wars would not end, Tamara decided she would take it upon herself to document atrocities committed by the Russian army. She wanted faces. She would go to excavated graves, the aftermath of explosions - anywhere, really. She would take pictures of faces and bodies, muddied and bloody.

She pulled the photo album from her bag. It was one of those family-vacation albums, gold leaf etching the blue plastic cover.

Look, look at the first page. A man is lying against a steering wheel. The front of the white car he sits in is crushed like a cola can. Part of his head is caved in. One eye is open. His shirt looks clean except for the blood that has dripped onto his collar. I didn't know that fresh blood is the same color as maraschino cherries. I turn the page and it is a visual feast of death and the macabre. Pages of decomposing corpses . . . body after body after body after body. After a while, despite my efforts, they became a mass of excruciating anonymity.

2/1 Kutuzovsky prospect, Moscow, Russia Telephone: +7 (495) 933-68-01 Fax: +7 (495) 933-68-39

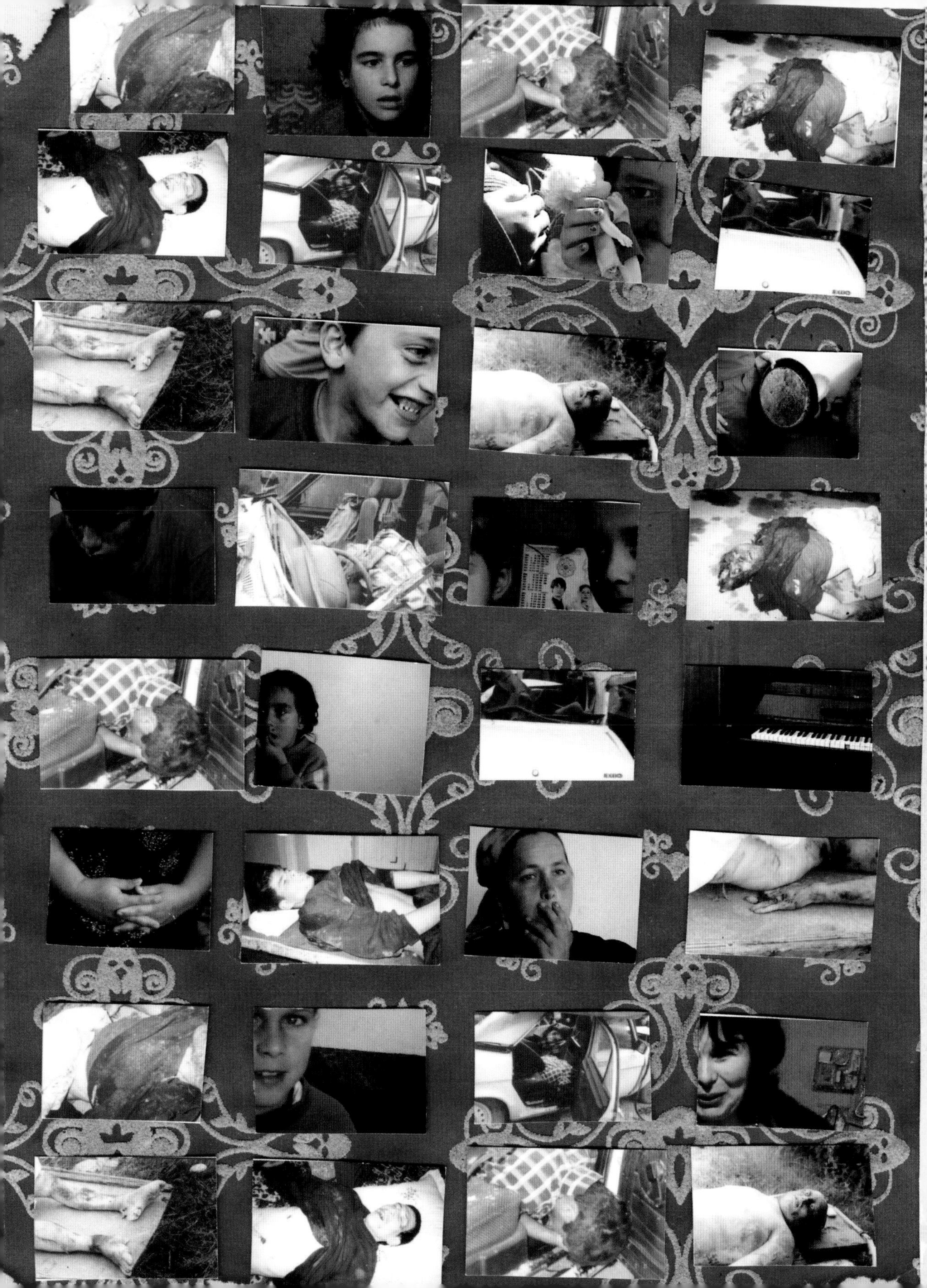

As Tamara turns the pages, I look up at her face. Tired, she looks like a girl who was trying to climb a mossy wall in the rain. She tells me that she will show these pictures to anyone, everyone, so that they might understand. I come across a picture of a little girl who looks like a Romanov princess. She stands in a bluish room. Next to her is a missile. It's not natural, her just standing there. Someone must have placed her beside the bomb in order to illustrate the menacing possibilities of this war. Didn't the photographer think that at any instant the bomb could explode, decimating both of them? Was life now a tightrope no matter what?

Tamara wants to give me this photo album to take home with me. What would I do with it? Most people I know are like me and would prefer to look away. I tell her that I can't take the album. That it's too precious. I can feel my brutality and dismissiveness disgusting both her and myself.

Curled, yellowed photos. In front of
wooden boxcars, I see old men hunched in
black overcoats and boys with their eyes
fixed on smoke in the sky. I see piles of
shoes, lamps, hats, gloves.
Turn the page.

There is no dignity in these pictures. Just human remains. Just this quiet, soulless end.

What do I do about the fact that I'm going home to try to forget what I have seen? I want to worry about my hair turning gray, or if the blue of my bedroom is really the perfect shade in north-facing light.